MW01028782

READING BACKWARDS

Figural Christology and the Fourfold Gospel Witness

Richard B. Hays

BAYLOR UNIVERSITY PRESS

© 2014 by Baylor University Press
Waco, Texas 76798-7363

Cover Design by Alyssa Stepien
Book Design by Diane Smith

Library of Congress Cataloging-in-Publication Data

Hays, Richard B.
  Reading backwards : figural Christology and the fourfold gospel witness /
Richard B. Hays.
  177 pages cm
  Includes bibliographical references and index.
  ISBN 978-1-4813-0232-6 (hardback : alk. paper)
  1. Bible. Gospels—Criticism, interpretation, etc. 2. Bible. Gospels—
Relation to the Old Testament. I. Title.
  BS2555.52.H39 2014
  226'.06--dc23
                                    2014024649

Printed in the United States of America on acid-free paper with a minimum
of 30 percent post-consumer waste recycled content.

To Chris,
who reads Israel's Scripture through different intertextual lenses,
with insight and wisdom.

θεοῦ γάρ ἐσμεν συνεργοί
1 Cor 3:9

Contents

PREFACE

For the past few years, whenever anyone would ask me what I was working on, my half-jesting answer was: "I'm working on a book on *Echoes of Scripture in the Gospels.*" The answer was half serious because I have indeed long been occupied with writing a Gospel-focused sequel to my earlier work *Echoes of Scripture in the Letters of Paul.*[1] But the answer was also half jesting because anyone who has explored this area of study realizes how impossible is the task of accounting for the vast intertextual network of scriptural citations, allusions, and echoes in the four canonical Gospels. My larger project, long in germination, remains unfinished—not only because of the daunting scope of the task, but also because of the constraints imposed on my time and energy during the past four years by my current position as dean of Duke Divinity School. The present small book, however, may be taken as a sort of progress report or as an *arrabōn* that looks in hope toward the ultimate promise of a more wide-ranging study. In the present work, therefore, I am seeking to distill a few narrowly focused insights about the fourfold witness of the Gospels to the divine identity of Jesus, viewed in light of their intertextual engagement with Israel's Scripture.

The six chapters of this book were originally delivered as the Hulsean Lectures in the Faculty of Divinity at Cambridge University during the fall of 2013 and the spring of 2014. The text of the lectures has been lightly revised, with a few notes added, but I have retained many of the features of the original oral delivery, with only modest adaptations to the demands of the printed page.

The reader of this book may be assisted by a few preliminary point-ers about what the book is and is not. I shall begin with the negatives. First of all, this is not a book about "the historical Jesus" or an attempt to reconstruct how Jesus of Nazareth interpreted Scripture or understood his own vocation and identity. Second, this is not a book about the social context of the communities that produced, received, and transmitted the traditions found in the Gospels; nor does the book attempt to argue for any particular hypothesis about a scribal school or about the social loca-tion of the authors of the Gospel texts. Third, this is not a book about *how* the early Christian communities came to develop their remarkable beliefs about Jesus as the embodiment of the God of Israel.[2]

Instead, this *is* a book that offers an account of the narrative rep-resentation of Jesus in the canonical Gospels, with particular attention to the ways in which the four Evangelists reread Israel's Scripture, as well as the ways in which Israel's Scripture prefigures and illuminates the central character in the Gospel stories. It is, in short, an exercise in intertextual close reading. Such a reading may offer fresh perspectives that might prove helpful in exploring the difficult historical questions outlined in the previous paragraph, but that is not the aim of the present study. These are questions that I must leave for another day.

One possible critique of the approach taken in this book might go something like this: Does this approach to the Evangelists as authors engaged in intertextual narration presuppose an anachronistic view of the Gospel writers as creative literary geniuses? Were the Evangelists con-sciously manipulating snippets of preexisting traditions to craft their own clever imaginative fictions? A concern of this kind was articulated by my friend and colleague Markus Bockmuehl in an incisive private communi-cation responding to some of the ideas found in the present book:

> I wonder if there may not be an equally important dynamic whose force operates the other way. It seems both a matter of fact and part of the biblical authors' intent that their engagement with the Old Testament is at least as much a function of the text's own agency in terms of its (divine) claim and impact on them, rather than merely of their "use" of it. Could one say that that they speak as they do because they are thunderstruck by the pressure that Scripture *as a hermeneutical Other* exerts on their own view of things? In other words, perhaps what seems to the critic as a device or strategy of manipulation may have seemed to the authors mere

faithfulness to the divine word's strong naming of the fresh reality God
had worked in their midst.[3]

I cite Bockmuehl's cautionary counterpoint chiefly in order to endorse
it and to clarify that I do not want to be understood as suggesting that
the Evangelists were engaged in fanciful Promethean poetic creativity.
Indeed, as Bockmuehl proposes, they may indeed have been "thunder-
struck" by the paradigm-shattering implications of their fresh encounter
with Israel's Scripture in light of the story of Jesus. (This is particularly
true of Mark.) As long ago as my *Echoes* book, I was fumbling toward
articulating something like this by arguing that Paul's interpretation of
the Old Testament was an instance of "dialectical," rather than "heuristic," intertextuality:

> The difference between these modes of imitation lies in the extent to
> which the subtext is finally allowed by the poet to retain its own voice, to
> answer back, to challenge the poet's own attempt at integration. . . . [T]he
> precursor goes on speaking in the derivative text. . . . Paul's proclamation
> needs the blessing of Scripture, and Scripture's witness . . . stands in judg-
> ment of all formulations of the gospel. On the other hand, Scripture's
> witness gains its eschatological coherence only in light of the gospel.[4]

Just this sort of dialectical interaction is hard-wired into the practice of
figural interpretation that is characteristic of the hermeneutics of the
Evangelists.[5] It will be the burden of the lectures contained in the present
book to illustrate how this dialectic operates in the Gospel narratives.

Another way of putting this point is to say that the Gospel narratives are not simply artful edifying fictions; rather, they are *testimony*.
The aim of these lectures is to listen carefully to their acts of narrative
witness-bearing and to discern the ways in which their testimony is the
product of a catalytic fusion of Israel's Scripture and the story of Jesus.

The plan of the book is simple. An introductory chapter frames the
issues. Then there is one chapter on each of the four Gospels, seeking to
listen to the distinctive voice of each and delineating the ways in which
they draw upon Scripture—both explicitly and implicitly—in their narrative depiction of Jesus' identity. (Biblical quotations follow the NRSV
except where I have supplied my own translations.) A final chapter then
reflects on the similarities and differences in the Gospels' hermeneutical
approaches to the task of telling the Gospel story. What are the benefits

and dangers of each of the four strategies of narration? What do they share in common, and what tensions might distinguish them? Finally, can we read Israel's Scripture in the same ways they did?

It has become a commonplace of Gospel studies in modernity to set John apart as a late text that reflects a more advanced stage of doctrinal development and a "higher" Christology. At an earlier stage of reflection, I pondered whether to focus these lectures on the Synoptic Gospels and to leave John out of the mix, perhaps reserving the Fourth Gospel for a subsequent study. But the more deeply I became engaged with the Synoptics, the more the conviction grew on me that their common witness to the divine identity of Jesus belonged closely together with John's witness. To be sure, John has his own distinctive narrative idiom and style, but at the end of day, John joins in chorus with the testimony of Mark, Matthew, and John that Jesus was not only the Son of God but actually the embodiment of the divine presence in the world. For that reason, to exclude John from these lectures would be to occlude an important aspect of the fourfold Gospel witness and to perpetuate a critical convention that, theologically considered, obscures more than it reveals. And so, these lectures follow the lead of the early church fathers, Irenaeus above all, in affirming both the legitimacy of figural interpretation of Israel's Scripture and the complementarity of the four Evangelists. Indeed, I now think that these two affirmations are hermeneutically intertwined as one unbreakable cord.

If the structural design of the book is straightforward, its interpretative methodology is only slightly less so. These lectures presuppose that all four canonical Gospels are deeply embedded in a symbolic world shaped by the Old Testament—or, to put the point in a modern critical idiom, that their "encyclopedia of production" is constituted in large measure by Israel's Scripture. (This does not mean that the symbolic world of Greco-Roman pagan antiquity is insignificant for the Gospels, but that it is secondary; the Evangelists' constructive christological affirmations are derived chiefly from hermeneutical appropriation and transformation of Israel's sacred texts and traditions.) Therefore, within the frame of cultural knowledge provided by the stories and prayers of Israel's Scripture, the Gospels gesture toward the meaning of Jesus' life, death, and resurrection by quoting or evoking scriptural texts. This means that a discerning interpretation of a Gospel text will often require recovery and exploration of these precursor texts.

This is not some arcane theory-driven methodology. It is a matter of simple attention to the way that human language and storytelling ordinarily work. I offer a couple of contemporary examples.

The investment wizard Warren Buffett, in the aftermath of a catastrophic economic downturn, wrote a letter to his shareholders advising them to adopt a cautious attitude toward the optimistic projections of economists and investment rating agencies. Here is how he phrased his counsel: "Beware of geeks bearing formulas."[6] The rhetorical punch of the line, of course, derives from its resonance with the common English proverb "Beware of Greeks bearing gifts," which is a paraphrase of Laocoön's famous line from Book 2 of Vergil's *Aeneid*: *timeo Danaos et dona ferentes* ("I fear the Greeks even when they are bearing gifts"). Buffett's wording was more than a cute echo of a common phrase; it carried particular weight because he was warning against false promises of economic benefit for those who bought into complex derivatives—that is, warning against accepting a gift that was in fact booby-trapped with dire danger, like the Trojan Horse in Vergil's story. No doubt many readers of Buffett's letter caught the drift of his counsel but failed to recognize its full clever evocation of the narrative from the *Aeneid*.

A second example—in his eloquent victory speech on the night of his initial election to the presidency of the United States, Barack Obama declared that his hearers could put their hands "on the arc of history and bend it once more toward the hope of a better day." The phrase echoed a maxim from the speeches of Martin Luther King Jr.: "The arc of the moral universe is long, but it bends toward justice." Certainly Obama's declaration was not a direct quotation of King. But just as certainly it was an audible echo that summoned his audience to take up once again the moral legacy of the American civil rights struggle and to renew their efforts to work for a just society.[7]

Examples of this kind could be multiplied endlessly because our discourse is inherently intertexual and allusive. In order to catch the full semantic force of the language in the examples just given, readers would have to hear the echoes of earlier texts and think backwards—from Buffett to Vergil, or from Obama to King—to grasp the relevant and illuminating parallels. The language of the Gospels works in the same way. A careful interpretation of the Gospel stories will require patient attention to their evocation of intertexts from Israel's Scripture.[8]

As we examine the intrabiblical intertextuality of the Gospels, we will frequently find that the language of the Evangelists resonates most strongly with the language of the Old Greek versions of Israel's Scripture, commonly referred to as the Septuagint (LXX), rather than with the Masoretic Hebrew texts (MT). This is hardly surprising, since the Evangelists were writing in Greek for Greek-reading audiences. In the concluding chapter, I will offer a brief reflection on this state of affairs. The format of these lectures does not permit an in-depth study of this phenomenon, but readers will find that with some frequency I have referred to the Greek, rather than the Hebrew, text of the Old Testament.[9]

Another technical problem that receives only glancing attention in these pages is the question of the possible literary dependence among the Gospels themselves—a different sort of intertextuality. This complex problem has not been the chief topic of my inquiry, but I owe the reader at least a cursory explanation of my working understanding of the issue. I share the consensus position of the majority of NT scholars that the Gospel of Mark is the earliest of the four canonical Gospels and that both Matthew and Luke drew upon Mark as a source. I do not, however, place any weight on the hypothesis that Matthew and Luke independently made use of a hypothetical common source, designated as "Q." There is no extant manuscript of such a source, nor is there any reference to it in the surviving documents of earliest Christianity. It seems to me equally probable—indeed more probable—that Luke knew Matthew and that the verbal agreements between these two Gospels can be explained in this fashion rather than through positing a hypothetical Q source.[10] But as the reader of these lectures will see, the interpretations developed here do not depend on a resolution of this classic problem in NT studies. Instead, the chapters that follow will seek to read each of the four Gospels with a view to the OT intertexts that it evokes and to ask how these intertexts function within the literary and theological construction of that individual Gospel. If we knew for certain that Luke used Matthew as a source, we could draw more specific conclusions on some points. But the nature of the evidence does not permit certainty, and we can go a long way in reading Luke and Matthew without appealing to any particular theory of their sources, beyond the recognition of their use of Mark and of the OT.

One concern that arose repeatedly in questions from the audience during the presentation of these lectures in Cambridge is how the argument set forth in these pages might impact conversations between Christians and Jews. Does a theological affirmation of the christological exegesis of Israel's Scriptures de facto invalidate Judaism and generate a hostile supersessionist understanding of the relationship between Israel and the church? The question is both important and complicated. I have not attempted in these lectures to solve the thorny problems surrounding Jewish-Christian dialogue. But it is my hope that the exegetical observations contained in the present book might actually promote constructive dialogue by clarifying how deeply rooted early "divine identity Christology" was in Israel's Scripture. It is particularly important to see that the sort of figural interpretation practiced by the canonical Evangelists is not a rejection but a retrospective hermeneutical transformation of Israel's sacred texts. Figural readings do not annihilate the earlier pole of the figural correspondence; to the contrary they affirm its reality and find in it a significance beyond that which anyone could previously have grasped. This recognition will not dissolve disagreements between Jews and Christians over the interpretation of Israel's Scripture, but it will at least clarify what is at issue and, in the best of cases, encourage respectful controversy between divided communities that both seek to serve the one God proclaimed in the *Shema*.

Although this book is lightly annotated, I would be remiss if I did not acknowledge from the beginning some of the important precursors for the work I am pursuing here. When one begins to survey the secondary literature on the interpretation of the OT in the NT, it quickly becomes apparent that countless learned studies have been written by many, many scholars—a great multitude that no one could count, from every nation, from all tribes and peoples and languages. Therefore, I have made no attempt even to approximate a comprehensive cataloging of the pertinent literature; I offer my apologies in advance to the many authors whose work I have read with profit over the past twelve years who are not cited in the sparse endnotes of the present book. Still, a few authors stand out as important influences on my understanding of the subjects treated in these Hulsean Lectures. I name them here in a cursory roll call, with appreciation even for those from whose interpretations I finally must dissent in one way or another.

C. H. Dodd's classic study *According to the Scriptures* is in several ways both an inspiration and a model for the present book: an inspiration because of its attention to the crucial role of scriptural interpretation in the formation of early Christian proclamation, and a model because of its concise brevity as a published lecture series.[11] Particularly significant was Dodd's demonstration that the NT authors' quotations of biblical texts often presupposed knowledge of the wider context from which they were drawn. **Barnabas Lindars** also studied the ways in which the early apostolic preaching coalesced around scriptural themes, though he overemphasized its reactive, apologetic function and undervalued its constructive narratival role.[12] **Nils A. Dahl**, one of my influential teachers when I was an M.Div. student at Yale in the 1970s, exemplified nuanced attention to the christological focus of early Christian exegesis in its Jewish context; and his student **Donald Juel**, in his book *Messianic Exegesis*, carried forward Dahl's legacy, particularly in his focus on the portrayal of Jesus as the crucified Messiah.[13] Don and I had a number of stimulating conversations about these matters before his untimely death in 2003, but we continued to disagree about the extent to which the NT's citations and allusions were evocative of the OT context of the cited passages; he contended for a more atomistic prooftexting approach.

On quite a different front, the work of **Hans Frei** had an enormous impact in encouraging me to recover the hermeneutical significance of the narrative depiction of the identity of Jesus in the Gospels. Hans was one of my early teachers and later my senior colleague on the faculty of Yale Divinity School. He did not undertake the sort of close intertextual readings that I seek to perform in the present book, nor did he give much attention to the individual voices of the canonical Evangelists. But he did powerfully remind theologians that the message of the Gospels is first of all to be found in the *narrative* rendering of the character of Jesus, not in a speculative reconstruction of events or communities behind the text.[14] It was also Frei who first introduced me to the learned and illuminating work of Erich Auerbach on figural interpretation. It will be evident to the reader of these lectures that Auerbach's analysis of *figura* is foundational to my argument.

The work of **Joel Marcus** contributed a new level of depth and sophistication to the study of NT interpretation of the Old, first through his significant monograph *The Way of the Lord* and subsequently through his thoroughgoing two-volume Anchor Bible commentary on the Gospel of Mark.[15] In the early stages of my study of Mark, I found Joel's knowledge of ancient Jewish biblical interpretation an indispensable guide to the fascinating mysteries of Mark's exegesis. For the past thirteen years, I have been pleased to count him among my colleagues and conversation partners at Duke.

I turn now to mention some of the scholars who have had a major impact on my thinking about the specific question of the divine identity of Jesus in the Gospels. This has been a topic of animated conversation between **N. T. Wright** and me for many years. Tom's wide-ranging account of Jesus as the one in whom the return of Yahweh to Zion was enacted has provoked much controversy;[16] in my view, he has undoubtedly identified a theologically significant theme that appears in the Gospels, particularly Matthew. I do not, however, entirely share Tom's confidence in attributing this self-conception to the Jesus of history. But he has raised my consciousness about the shape of the problem and effectively highlighted some of the ways in which Jesus is in fact portrayed in the Synoptic narratives as the embodied manifestation of Israel's God.

Larry Hurtado is a leading figure among several scholars who have argued for a fresh consideration of the development of a "high Christology" at a very early stage of the history of the earliest church. His books *One God, One Lord* and *Lord Jesus Christ* have challenged the prevalent older theories of the *Religionsgeschichtliche Schule* about the late date and Hellenistic milieu of the origin of Christian beliefs about the divinity of Jesus.[17] Hurtado has highlighted the evidence for the worship of Jesus in Jewish congregations at an early date; he seeks to explain this as a "mutation" or "variant" of earlier Jewish reverence for angels or other "divine agents." As I have indicated, the present lectures do not investigate the question of the etiology of the Gospels' divine identity Christology. I would suggest, however, that Hurtado is certainly correct about the early date and Jewish milieu for this extraordinary development—even though I am not persuaded by his hypothesis about the derivation of the confession of Jesus' divine identity from earlier Jewish models.

It is **Richard Bauckham** who has most compellingly called for a radical rethinking of Jewish monotheism and pressed for recognition that the NT documents emphatically place Jesus on the divine side of the categorical distinction between Creator and creation. Bauckham's short book *God Crucified* (originally his Didsbury Lectures in Manchester) was for me an eye-opening work that forced me to rethink many things and opened up new lines of inquiry.[18] In the fall of 2008, I was privileged to participate with Richard in a joint presentation on "Divine Identity Christology," sponsored by Tyndale House, Cambridge. Richard spoke about the divine identity of Jesus in the Gospel of Mark, and I was given the task of speaking on divine identity Christology in Luke. At the time, I had only ill-formed thoughts and observations to offer, but this forum became an important springboard that ultimately propelled me toward the treatment of Luke found in chapter 4 of this book.

Daniel Boyarin is another scholar who has provocatively destabilized conventional beliefs about what first-century Jews could and could not have believed about multiplicity within the divine identity.[19] Approaching the question from his comprehensive knowledge of rabbinic and other Jewish texts, he has sought to demonstrate that a particular sort of "binitarianism," heavily indebted to exegesis of Daniel 7, was widespread in Jewish thought in the ancient Mediterranean world. On his reading, the rabbinic attempt to stigmatize such beliefs was a later development. Boyarin's illuminating interpretation of the prologue of the Fourth Gospel underlies part of my argument in chapter 5 of the present study.

My understanding of Lukan Christology was revolutionized by supervising the dissertation work of **C. Kavin Rowe**, who has documented the remarkable way in which Luke's Gospel creates a narrative identity of Jesus as "Lord"—an identity shared with the one God of Israel.[20] Even when he was my doctoral student, Kavin taught me a great deal. Now, as my faculty colleague at Duke, he continues to do so.

Finally, I must call attention to the privileged experience of participating in a three-year collaborative research project at the Center of Theological Inquiry in Princeton on "The Identity of Jesus." The colleagues in that extraordinary group all contributed to rich discussions that both expanded and deepened my understanding of the ways in which Scripture (Old and New Testament alike) and the church's theological tradition can illuminate the figure of Jesus. I am grateful to Wallace Alston and Robert Jenson at CTI for making this project possible.[21]

The mention of the Center of Theological Inquiry leads me into a long list of acknowledgments and words of thanks to the many people and institutions who have contributed to the development of the thoughts contained in this book. Given the brevity of the present work, I have accrued an uncommonly lengthy list of debts, both intellectual and practical. That is a result of the lamentably long process of germination to which I referred at the beginning of this preface.

First and most importantly I want to thank the Faculty of Divinity in Cambridge University for the invitation to deliver the Hulsean Lectures and for their flexibility in spreading the delivery of the lectures out over a period of six months to accommodate the demands of my administrative obligations at Duke. The lectures were delivered in three sets of two, on November 12–13, 2013; February 11–12, 2014; and April 29–30, 2014. I am grateful to Professor Eamon Duffy for the initial invitation to present the lectures and to Professor Duffy, Professor Judith Lieu, Professor David Ford, Dr. Simon Gathercole, and many other colleagues in Cambridge for their gracious hospitality during my visits there.

The Hulsean Lectures represented the distillation and focusing of topics I had discussed in many public forums over the preceding twelve years. I particularly want to thank four institutions for the opportunity to present material on these themes in major lectureships during the ten years prior to the Hulseans; all of these lectures prefigured in various ways the content of the present book. In 2004, I had the honor of delivering the Burns Lectures at the University of Otago in Dunedin, New Zealand; Professor Paul Trebilco was my gracious host during a two-week stay there. Four years later I presented the 2008 Sprunt Lectures at Union Theological Seminary in Richmond, Virginia. I offered a similar series for the Winter Pastors' Convocation at Truett Divinity School, Baylor University, in Waco, Texas, in 2011. And in 2012 I delivered the Gunning Lectures in the University of Edinburgh, Scotland. In each of these lectureships, I was given the opportunity to develop a broad overview of what it might mean to read the OT through the eyes of the Evangelists.

The four lectureships just noted offered the fullest anticipation of the Hulseans and the shape of the present book. But in recent years I have also lectured on many different occasions on various topics related to the interpretation of the OT in the Gospels. The list of institutions, both academic and ecclesial, where I have spoken about such matters is too long to include here, but I am grateful to the many friends, colleagues, and audiences who have engaged in conversation with me about the challenges of understanding the Evangelists as readers of Israel's Scriptures.

The research undergirding these lectures has been conducted with the aid of theological libraries in three places: Duke Divinity School;

Princeton Theological Seminary, during two stints in residence at the Center of Theological Inquiry, 2001–2002 and 2009; and Cambridge, England, where I spent a wonderful six months during 2008 and drew on the resources of the Tyndale House Library, the library of the Faculty of Divinity, and the Cambridge University Library. I would like to acknowledge with appreciation the assistance of knowledgeable library staff in each of these places. And I am also grateful to Clare Hall, Cambridge University, for granting me appointment as a visiting fellow during my stay in 2008 and subsequently electing me to life membership. Dean L. Gregory Jones of Duke Divinity School provided significant support for the research leave that enabled me to undertake that valuable and formative Cambridge sojourn.

Of the several doctoral students who have provided essential research assistance, I would like to mention four whose aid has been especially important to the current project. At Duke: David Moffitt, Hans Arneson, and Josh Leim; and at Princeton: Mary Schmitt. Though my progress on this work has been slow, it would have been slower without their help; the fruits of their labor will perhaps be more evident when I am finally able to produce the larger study of which this book is a foretaste.

Given the long period of rumination that went into this book, there have been many friends and colleagues who have read portions of it and offered helpful responses and suggestions. To list them all here would be impossible, but I would like to acknowledge a very few whose reading has been especially valuable to me. Tom Wright and Kavin Rowe read all, or nearly all, of the material that went into the Hulsean Lectures and gave wise and substantive feedback. Professor Clifton Black of Princeton Seminary read an early draft of a much lengthier chapter on Mark and made helpful comments. Professor Sarah Coakley of Cambridge also read a draft of the Mark material and, among her many stimulating responses, challenged me to be more direct and assertive about my claims concerning Jesus' divine identity in that Gospel. And Dr. Steve Walton consulted with me in a very helpful way during my residency in Cambridge about the theme of divine identity Christology in Luke. Similarly, in the fall of 2008, I was privileged to participate in twenty-one sessions with David Ford and Richard Bauckham in which the three of us read, chapter by chapter, the Greek text of the Gospel of John and discussed its interpretation. Though they did not read a draft of my chapter on John (which I had not even begun to write during the time of our meetings), our deliberations about the Fourth Gospel materially informed the work I was later to do on it. And I would be remiss to overlook the many wonderful conversations with my students at Duke Divinity School who participated in my seminars on the Old Testament in the New during the years I have been working on this project. Their questions and insights have deepened my understanding in more ways than I can consciously remember or adequately acknowledge.

Special thanks must go to Dr. Carey Newman, the director of Baylor University Press, who has for many years sought to cajole my big book on the Gospels out of me, and who graciously and eagerly accepted my proposal to publish the Hulsean Lectures as a little book, an offering of firstfruits in anticipation of a fuller harvest to come. Carey has voraciously read everything I have sent him over the years and has vigorously engaged with it, offering many very helpful suggestions. He has even hospitably initiated me into membership in the Early High Christology Club, even though in the present book I argue that we should stop talking about "high" and "low" Christologies in the canonical Gospels.

On a personal note, words fail me to express my deep gratitude to my wife and soulmate, Judy, who has endured many years of marriage to a husband attempting to juggle research, writing, administration, and a family life, often unsuccessfully. It was Judy who, after hearing me deliver the second of the Hulsean lectures, said to me, in the privacy of our guest room in Clare Hall, "You need to publish this *now*." That exhortation was not only an outpouring of her justified impatience but also a measured expression of her sharp editorial judgment. I am grateful for her endless love and for the companionship we have shared during forty-four years of an amazing journey together.

This book is dedicated to our son Christopher B. Hays, now the D. Wilson Moore Associate Professor of Ancient Near Eastern Studies at Fuller Theological Seminary. He comes to the reading of Israel's Scripture from a deep knowledge of the languages and culture of the Ancient Near East.[22] And so the echoes that he hears there are very different from the ones sketched in these lectures. But he is an incisive reader who understands poetry and texts. I dedicate this book to him with great affection and in appreciation for his love of language and his passion for reading Scripture well.

It is my hope that readers of this book may be moved and encouraged to return to the reading of Scripture with fresh perspective, to read closely and imaginatively, and to read backwards along with the Evangelists.

Richard B. Hays
Durham, North Carolina
Pentecost, 2014

1

"The Manger in Which Christ Lies"

Figural Readings of Israel's Scriptures

Reading Scripture through the Eyes of the Evangelists?

When Martin Luther published his German translation of the Pentateuch in 1523, he composed a preface explaining why his German readers should value the Old Testament. Presumably then, as now, there was some tendency in the churches to denigrate or disregard Israel's Scripture in favor of the allegedly more pure and spiritual New Testament. Here is what Luther wrote:

> There are some who have little regard for the Old Testament. They think of it as a book that was given to the Jewish people only and is now out of date, containing only stories of past times. . . . But Christ says in John 5, "Search the Scriptures, for it is they that bear witness to me." . . . [T]he Scriptures of the Old Testament are not to be despised but diligently read. . . . Therefore dismiss your own opinions and feelings and think of the Scriptures as the loftiest and noblest of holy things, as the richest of mines which can never be sufficiently explored, in order that you may find that divine wisdom which God here lays before you in such simple guise as to quench all pride. Here you will find the swaddling cloths and the manger in which Christ lies. . . . Simple and lowly are these swaddling cloths, but dear is the treasure, Christ, who lies in them.[1]

"The manger in which Christ lies"—it is a striking image, a vivid trope of the sort that Luther relished. What is Luther doing here? He is reading the Lukan birth story *figurally*, employing the manger as a metaphor for the manner in which the Old Testament contains Jesus Christ. Just as Jesus was wrapped in humble swaddling cloths in the manger, so too is he wrapped in the swaddling cloths of the Law, the Prophets, and the Writings.

We might put it this way: Luther is reading the New Testament figurally in order to proclaim the legitimacy of a figural reading of the Old. Only if we frame the question this way, only if we embrace figural interpretation, can we make sense of the Gospel of John's assertion that the Scriptures bear witness to Jesus Christ. He is the treasure who lies figurally wrapped in the folds of the OT. But if he is wrapped, that suggests he is not only contained but also partly concealed within the manger. It is the task of a figural reading first to enter the humble surroundings of the stable, as did the shepherds in Bethlehem, but then also to *"search the Scriptures"*—to read backwards to unwind the swaddling cloths and to disclose the Christ who lies there.

That is the task before us in these Hulsean Lectures: to search out some of the ways in which the four canonical Evangelists unwind the swaddling cloths—that is, the various ways in which they read Israel's Scripture. One result of this inquiry will be to disclose that all four of them, in interestingly distinct ways, embody and enact the sort of figural christological reading that Luther commends. (Indeed, it would seem that Luther learned this figural hermeneutical strategy precisely from the Evangelists; he dares to proclaim that the Old Testament is "the manger in which Christ lies" precisely because the Evangelists have taught him to read Scripture metaphorically.)

But what do I mean by "figural interpretation"? Here is Erich Auerbach's classic definition:

> Figural interpretation establishes a connection between two events or persons in such a way that the first signifies not only itself but also the second, while the second involves or fulfills the first. The two poles of a figure are separated in time, but both, being real events or persons, are within temporality. They are both contained in the flowing stream which is historical life, and only the comprehension, the *intellectus spiritualis*, of their interdependence is a spiritual act.[2]

There is consequently a significant difference between *prediction* and *prefiguration*. Figural reading need not presume that the OT authors—or the characters they narrate—were conscious of predicting or anticipating Christ. Rather, the discernment of a figural correspondence is necessarily retrospective rather than prospective. (Another way to put this point is that figural reading is a form of intertextual interpretation that focuses on an intertextuality of *reception* rather than of *production*.)[3] The act of retrospective recognition is the *intellectus spiritualis*. Because the two poles of a figure are events within "the flowing stream" of time, the correspondence can be discerned only after the second event has occurred and imparted a new pattern of significance to the first. But once the pattern of correspondence has been grasped, the semantic force of the figure flows both ways, as the second event receives deeper significance from the first. Building on Auerbach's work, the most concise and illuminating analysis of figural reading in the Christian theological tradition remains that of Hans Frei, in *The Eclipse of Biblical Narrative*.[4] As Frei observes, a hermeneutical strategy that relies on figural interpretation of the Bible creates deep theological coherence within the biblical narrative, for it "sets forth the unity of the canon as a single cumulative and complex pattern of meaning."[5]

But, of course, this kind of reading has been distinctly out of fashion since the advent of modern historical criticism. Indeed, one reason for modernity's incredulity toward the Christian faith (an incredulity that has been repeatedly taken to the bank by the authors of breathless bestsellers) is the charge that Christian proclamation rests on twisted and tendentious misreadings of the Hebrew Scriptures.

These alleged misreadings, however, are not late or incidental developments within Christian thought; rather, the claim that the events of Jesus' life, death, and resurrection took place "according to the Scriptures" stands at the heart of the NT's message. All four canonical Gospels declare that the Torah and the Prophets and the Psalms mysteriously prefigure Jesus. The author of the Fourth Gospel puts the claim succinctly: in the same passage in John 5 to which Luther pointed, Jesus declares, "If you believed Moses, you would believe me, for he wrote about me" (John 5:46).

But modern historical criticism characteristically judges, to the contrary, that the NT's christological readings of Israel's Scripture are simply a big mistake: they twist and misrepresent the original sense of the texts. To cite a single example, consider the following quotation from the distinguished German NT scholar Udo Schnelle, in his *Theology of the New Testament*: "A 'biblical theology' is not possible because: (1) the Old Testament is *silent* about Jesus Christ, [and] (2) the resurrection from the dead *of one who was crucified* cannot be integrated into any ancient system of meaning formation."[6] Notice that both of these reasons adduced by Schnelle for the impossibility of a biblical theology directly contradict the explicit testimony of the NT writers themselves! They emphatically do not think the OT is silent about Jesus Christ, and they assert that the resurrection of Jesus from the dead actually provides the hermeneutical clue that decisively integrates Israel's entire "system of meaning formation."[7] It is a particularly poignant irony that Schnelle holds the chair as Professor of New Testament at the University of Halle-Wittenberg: the geographical proximity of Professor Schnelle to Luther's home base accentuates the hermeneutical distance traveled by biblical scholarship since the sixteenth century.[8]

Let us consider another example closer to our own personal experience in the academy. Here is a question for those of you who have at some point during the past fifty years been asked to write an exegesis paper on a passage in the Pentateuch: What grade would you have received if you had turned in an essay on, say, Exodus 12 contending that the Passover story is really all about Jesus?

My point is this: the reading strategies of historical criticism—strategies that are themselves historically contingent—have created a cluster of quandaries for Christian theology. Why do the Gospel writers read Scripture in such surprising ways? Does Christian faith require the illegitimate theft of someone else's sacred texts? The full depth of these problems is too rarely explored in our theology.

Over the course of these lectures, I want to contend that the Gospel writers summon us to a conversion of the imagination. I want to suggest to you that we will learn to read Scripture rightly only if our minds and imaginations are opened by seeing the scriptural text—and therefore the world—through the Evangelists' eyes. In order to explore that hermeneutical possibility, we must give close consideration to the revisionary figural ways that the four Gospel writers actually read Israel's Scripture. So our governing heuristic questions will be these: How does each of the Evangelists read Israel's Scripture? How does each one draw upon figural interpretation of the Old Testament to depict the identity of Jesus and to interpret his significance? Here is a preliminary preview of what we will find as we pursue our exploration: *the Gospels teach us how to read the OT, and—at the same time—the OT teaches us how to read the Gospels.* Or, to put it a little differently, we learn to read the OT by *reading backwards* from the Gospels, and—at the same time—we learn how to read the Gospels by *reading forwards* from the OT.

I am aware that each of the two parts of this thesis is, in its own way, unfashionable. Many would say that to speak of the NT teaching us to read the OT is to get things backwards, a bit like Persse McGarrigle, the young English professor in David Lodge's comic novel *Small World*, who plans to write a book about the influence of T. S. Eliot on Shakespeare![9] I shall return to this objection later in the lecture.

But first let us attend to the latter claim—that the OT teaches us how to read the Gospels—a claim perhaps less scandalous than the former. There is a certain obvious sense in which the Gospels arise out of the religious and cultural matrix of the OT. Jesus and his first followers were Jews whose symbolic world was shaped by Israel's Scripture: their categories for interpreting the world and their hopes for God's saving action were fundamentally conditioned by the biblical stories of God's dealings with the people Israel. Therefore, it is not surprising that as the earliest Christian communities began to tell and retell stories about Jesus, they interpreted his life, death, and resurrection in relation to those biblical stories (i.e., the texts that Christians later came to call the Old Testament). The authors of our four canonical Gospels were the heirs of this tradition of storytelling, and they shared the early Christian community's passionate concern—a concern that, as far as we can tell, goes back to Jesus himself—to show that Jesus' teachings and actions, as well as his violent death and ultimate vindication, constituted the continuation and climax of the ancient biblical story.

Nonetheless, many "mainstream" Protestant churches today are in fact naively Marcionite in their theology and practice: in their worship services they have no OT reading, or if the OT is read it is rarely preached upon. Judaism is regarded as a legalistic foil from which Jesus has delivered us. (I once had a student say to me in class: "Judaism was a harsh religion that taught people to *fear* God's judgment, but Jesus came to teach us to *love* God with all our heart and soul and strength.")[10] This unconscious Marcionite bias has had a disastrous effect on the theological imagination of many Protestant churches, at least in the United States: everything in the Gospels that looks too much like the OT is screened out as "inauthentic" and theologically dangerous—teachings about the election of a particular people, the mandate for holiness and purity, the expectation of God's ultimate judgment of the world. All this is excluded from the authentic red-letter material of what Jesus "really" taught.

This is the sort of thing Dietrich Bonhoeffer had in mind when he wrote, near the end of his life, about the crucial importance of having our lives and our understanding grounded in the Old Testament: "Whoever would too quickly and too directly be and feel in accordance with the New Testament is, in my opinion, no Christian."[11] (Of course, in Bonhoeffer's historical setting, he was locked in a life-and-death struggle with a heretical and malevolent "German Christianity" that sought to cut Christianity loose from its Jewish roots.) In the spirit of Bonhoeffer's admonition, it will be profitable to spend some time first exploring how the OT teaches us to read the Gospels before we return to the more provocative question of how the Gospels teach us to read the OT.

How Does the OT Teach Us to Read the Gospels?

For purposes of illustration, I want to begin with two examples from the Gospel of Mark. How might the OT teach us to read each of these passages more penetratingly?

Prophetic action in the Temple (Mark 11:15-19). We begin with Mark 11:15-19, the climactic scene in the Temple where Jesus, in an act of prophetic street theater, overturns the tables of the moneychangers. A full reading of the event requires careful attention to the commentary provided by Jesus' words in the Temple after driving out the merchants and moneychangers, commentary in which we find a fusion of OT texts from Isaiah and Jeremiah.

> Is it not written,
> *"My house shall be called a house of prayer for all nations"?*
> But you have made it *a den of robbers.* (Mark 11:17)

The first quotation, from Isaiah 56:7, belongs originally to Isaiah's vision of an eschatologically restored Jerusalem in which God's deliverance has been revealed (56:1). One salient feature of this redeemed order is that *Gentiles* will come to Mount Zion to worship alongside God's people:

> These [foreigners] I will bring to my holy mountain,
> and make them joyful in my house of prayer;
> their burnt offerings and sacrifices
> will be accepted on my altar;
> *for my house shall be called a house of prayer*
> *for all nations.*
> Thus says the Lord GOD,
> who gathers the outcasts of Israel,

I will gather others to them
besides those already gathered. (Isa 56:7-8)

By citing this passage, Mark portrays Jesus' protest action as an indictment of the Temple authorities for turning the Temple into a bazaar, cluttering the outer "court of the Gentiles" and making it unsuitable as a place of worship for the Gentile "others" who might want to gather there to pray. By driving out the merchants, Mark's Jesus clears the way, figuratively, for the restored worship of the kingdom of God, in which all nations will participate along with the returning exiles of Israel. Thus, Jesus' action looks forward to the eschatological redemption of Jerusalem.[12]

At the same time, Jesus' accusation that, in contrast to the eschatological vision, the Temple authorities have made God's house "a den of robbers" (σπήλαιον λῃστῶν) alludes forcefully to Jeremiah's Temple sermon (Jer 7:1–8:3). In this well-known passage, God instructs Jeremiah to "stand in the gate of the Lord's house" and deliver a scathing denunciation and prophecy of destruction. In order to appreciate the force of the "den of robbers" allusion, let us recall the context in which Jeremiah first used this arresting phrase:

> Thus says the Lord of hosts, the God of Israel: Amend your ways and your doings, and let me dwell with you in this place. Do not trust in these deceptive words: "This is the temple of the Lord, the temple of the Lord, the temple of the Lord." . . .
>   Will you steal, murder, commit adultery, swear falsely, make offerings to Baal, and go after other gods that you have not known, and then come and stand before me in this house, which is called by my name, and say, "We are safe!"—only to go on doing all these abominations? Has this house, which is called by my name, become *a den of robbers* [LXX: σπήλαιον λῃστῶν] in your sight? (Jer 7:3-4, 9-11a)

Jeremiah's judgment oracle concludes with a declaration that the Lord intends to destroy the Temple (7:13-15). Consequently, when Jesus storms into the Temple, overturns the tables of the moneychangers, and invokes Jeremiah's image of the Temple as *a den of robbers*, there can be no doubt that the allusion is meant to recall the wider context of Jeremiah's prophetic tirade and that the action foreshadows the Temple destruction which is later specifically prophesied in Mark 13:1-2: "As he came out of the temple, one of his disciples said to him, 'Look, Teacher, what large stones and what large buildings!' Then Jesus asked him, 'Do you see these great buildings? Not one stone will be left here upon another; all will be thrown down.'"

E. P. Sanders has forcefully argued the case that Jesus' demonstration in the Temple was a prophetic action symbolizing its destruction. Oddly, however, he dismisses the Jeremiah allusion in 11:17 as secondary and inauthentic. Indeed, he suggests that the Evangelists have used the quotation about the "den of robbers" to cover up the embarrassing historical fact of Jesus' threat of destruction and to "make it appear that Jesus was quite reasonably protesting against dishonesty."[13] Sanders does not consider the possibility that the Jeremiah allusion has precisely the effect of signifying the Temple's impending destruction—which is what Jeremiah prophesied to his generation. I think this apparent oversight is to be explained by Sanders' overriding concern to reject anachronistic Protestant interpretations of Jesus' action as a call for reform, "cleansing" the Temple of its allegedly disgusting practices of animal sacrifice.[14] While accepting Sanders' critique of such readings, we may also suggest that Sanders' argument for interpreting the Temple action as a prophecy of destruction would actually be strengthened by attending to the specific original context in Jeremiah of the "den of robbers" allusion. The allusion carries, quite simply, an ominous threat of judgment and destruction. This line of thought would certainly hold good for the analysis of Mark's theology, and I see no reason to deny that the historical figure of Jesus might well have patterned his words and actions after the prophet Jeremiah.[15]

Just in case we might miss the allusion to Jeremiah, however, Mark provides one more telling clue: the cursing of the fig tree (Mark 11:12-14, 20-21) frames Jesus' Temple action with an enacted parable of destruction for the unfaithful, unfruitful nation. And the story of the withered fig tree explicitly echoes the judgment oracle found in Jeremiah 8:13:

> When I wanted to gather them, says the Lord,
> there are no grapes on the vine,
> nor figs on the fig tree;
> even the leaves are withered,
> and what I gave them has passed away from them.

Thus, Mark's narrative casts Jesus in typological relation to Jeremiah. Just as Jeremiah had spoken of Israel as an unfruitful, withered fig tree, Jesus performs a symbolic tree-withering act that prefigures the fate of

Israel—or, at least, of the Temple. Just as Jeremiah condemned the prophets and priests who spoke false deceptive words of peace and comfort while practicing injustice and idolatry, so Jesus takes up the mantle of Jeremiah to condemn the Temple establishment once again. The phrase "den of robbers" and the image of the barren fig tree provide the imaginative links; for the reader who grasps the figural connection, the outward-rippling implications are clear. As judgment fell upon Israel in Jeremiah's time, so it looms once again over the Temple.[16]

Thus, Jesus' action in the Temple acquires its full significance only when we are taught by the OT to understand it in relation to the prophetic words of Isaiah and Jeremiah. Note carefully that neither Isaiah nor Jeremiah *prophesied* Jesus' turning over of the tables of the moneychangers. (We find here no formula quotation: "He did these things in order to fulfill what was written in the prophet.") Rather, Jesus' action acquires its intelligibility when it is set in a dialectical *intertextual* relation *both* to Isaiah's vision of a restored Jerusalem *and* to Jeremiah's word of judgment against the city and its Temple.

The parable of the Wicked Tenants. Let us turn now to consider somewhat more briefly a passage in which the OT's shaping of our reading is a little more allusive and indirect—but no less crucial for making sense of the narrative.

As we explore how the OT teaches us to read the Gospels, it is illuminating to compare the parable of the Wicked Tenants in its canonical synoptic versions (Mark 12:1-12 / Matt 21:33-46 / Luke 20:9-19) to the stripped-down version that appears in the extracanonical second-century Gospel of Thomas (GosT 65). The Gospel of Thomas systematically excludes all the resonant OT allusions that appear in the canonical tellings of the tale: the details about the planting and preparation of the vineyard that vividly recall Isaiah's Song of the Vineyard (Isa 5:1-7), the description of the vineyard owner's son as a "beloved son" (evocative of Gen 22:2; Ps 2:7; and Isa 42:1), the tenants' declaration, "Come, let us kill him" (echoing Joseph's brothers in Gen 37:20—the sentence in Greek [δεῦτε ἀποκτείνωμεν αὐτόν] is a verbatim citation of the Joseph story in the LXX text, a phrase not found anywhere else in the Greek Bible), and the concluding citation of Psalm 118:22-23, proclaiming that the stone the builders rejected has become the cornerstone (see fig. 1 following).[17]

FIGURE 1
OT Echoes in Mark 12:1-12, Contrasted with Gospel of Thomas 65–66

Mark 12:1-12	Gospel of Thomas 65–66
¹Then he began to speak to them in parables. *"A man planted a vineyard, put a fence around it, dug a pit for the wine press, and built a watchtower [Isa 5:2];* then he leased it to tenants and went to another country. ²When the season came, he sent a slave to the tenants to collect from them his share of the produce of the vineyard. ³But they seized him, and beat him, and sent him away empty-handed.	65 He said, A good man had a vineyard He gave it to tenants that they might cultivate it and he might receive its fruit from them. He sent his servant so that the tenants might give him the fruit of the vineyard. They seized his servant and beat him; a little more and they would have killed him. The servant came and told it to his master. His master said, Perhaps he did not know them.
⁴And again he sent another slave to them; this one they beat over the head and insulted. ⁵Then he sent another, and that one they killed. And so it was with many others; some they beat, and others they killed. ⁶He had still one other, *a beloved son [Gen 22:2; Ps 2:7; Isa 42:1].*	He sent another servant; the tenants beat him as well.
Finally he sent him to them, saying, 'They will respect my son.' ⁷But those tenants said to one another, 'This is the heir; **come, let us kill him [Gen 37:20],** and the inheritance will be ours.' ⁸So they seized him, killed him, and threw him out of the vineyard. ⁹What then will the owner of the vineyard do? He will come and destroy the tenants and give the vineyard to others. ¹⁰*Have you not read this scripture: 'The stone that the builders rejected has become the cornerstone;* ¹¹*this was the Lord's doing, and it is amazing in our eyes'? [Ps 118:22-23]"* ¹²When they realized that he had told this parable against them, they wanted to arrest him, but they feared the crowd. So they left him and went away.	Then the owner sent his son. He said, Perhaps they will respect my son. Since those tenants knew that he was the heir of the vineyard, they seized him and killed him. He who has ears, let him hear. 66 Jesus said: Show me the stone which the builders rejected. It is the cornerstone.

Some NT scholars have speculated that Thomas' expurgated version of the parable is more historically authentic than the canonical versions (i.e., closer to the teaching of the historical Jesus) because it is less allegorical.[18] In fact, however, the chief effect of Thomas' exclusions is to extract the parable from its Jewish historical setting, distancing it from the cultural and religious context in which Jesus lived and taught.[19] The canonical tellings, on the other hand, beckon the reader to recall Isaiah 5:7:

> For the vineyard of the Lord of Hosts is the house of Israel,
> and the people of Judah are his pleasant planting;
> he expected justice, but saw bloodshed;
> righteousness, but heard a cry!

By evoking this canonical memory, the Synoptic Gospels press us to interpret the parable as a word of judgment on the leaders of Israel for their failure to yield the vineyard's grapes to its rightful owner. The parable thereby places the story of Jesus within the unfolding story of Israel and presents his death as the climax of a pattern of unfaithfulness and judgment familiar to any reader of Israel's prophetic literature. The pattern is as old as the story of Joseph's resentful brothers.

At the same time, the identification of Jesus as the "beloved son" (Mark 12:6; Luke 20:13)—linking him both to Isaac (the beloved son whom Abraham was called to offer up to a sacrificial death) and to the Davidic king (the beloved son whose kingly rule is proclaimed in Ps 2:7-9)—hints that his death is to be understood not merely as a tragic episode of violence but as an event of saving significance for Israel. This intimation is confirmed by the culminating Psalm citation in the parable, which looks forward to the resurrection as God's saving act:

> The stone that the builders rejected
> has become the cornerstone;
> this was the Lord's doing,
> and it is amazing in our eyes. (Mark 12:10-11 par., citing Ps 118:22-23)

When this citation is linked to the echo of the story of Joseph, who was rescued from the pit and ascended to a position of power—a position from which he ultimately provided saving help to his own people—the resonance between Jesus' parable and Israel's Scripture is particularly powerful. Thus, the canonical synoptic versions situate the parable of the Wicked Tenants within a larger narrative context and present Jesus' death and resurrection as the climax of the story of Israel.

The Gospel of Thomas, by contrast, offers a colorless, enigmatic version of the parable that distances it from the story of Israel and leaves it open to be read however the reader may choose; in the case of Thomas, the parable is co-opted into a gnostic message of detachment from an evil world. Thus, Thomas' editorial de-Judaizing of the parable illustrates the loss of meaning—or, better, distortion of meaning—that occurs when the Gospel traditions are artificially removed from the canonical matrix of Israel's story. Thomas' stripped-down text is almost certainly historically secondary. The canonical tellings bear lively witness to a controversy internal to Jewish tradition, a controversy that was alive and well both in Jesus' lifetime and in the *Sitz im Leben* of the Evangelists: a controversy over who is the authentic caretaker and heir of Israel's traditions. Thomas, by contrast, dilutes the historical and narrative specificity of the material.[20] But the canonical Gospels evoke Israel's Scripture in order to provide both hermeneutical guidance and theological depth. The OT teaches us to read the parable with understanding.

———

These two examples demonstrate some of the ways that the OT teaches us to read the Gospels. Let me lift out just three salient points arising from these passages:

(1) The OT teaches us to take seriously God's word of judgment: those who oppress the alien, the widow, and the orphan and shed innocent blood will come under God's fearful judgment, whether in Jeremiah's Judah in the seventh century B.C.E., in Jerusalem in Jesus' lifetime, or in our own time. Those who reject the prophets that God sends—including even God's own Son—will suffer the loss of the vineyard that was entrusted to them. Likewise, those who devote their lives to idolatry while offering facile and superficial worship will come under the sentence of destruction and exile. Jesus does not defuse such judgment: he repeats and re-enacts it. The OT focuses our understanding of Jesus' role as an eschatological prophet of God's judgment. The sweet, infinitely inclusive Jesus meek and mild, so beloved by modern Protestantism, is a Jesus cut loose from his OT roots.

(2) The OT teaches us that all our prayer and action should be ordered toward Isaiah's vision of a restored and healed new creation; that is to say, the salvation proclaimed in the Gospels is neither merely individual nor otherworldly. In the passage from Mark 11 that we have considered, Jesus appeals to the OT to insist that our worship of God should make a space to prefigure God's eschatological gathering of the outcasts and the strangers. And in Mark 12, the citation of Psalm 118 adumbrates that the story of Israel will not end in violence and futility; the vineyard, under care of different hands, may yet flourish and yield fruit to its rightful owner.

(3) How will such a redemptive ending take place? The OT hints mysteriously that God's beloved Son will suffer rejection, suffer violence, and be cast into the Pit (prefigured in the stories of the binding of Isaac and the story of Joseph) but that he will also "become the head of the corner" as an exalted king (prefigured not only in the happy endings of the Isaac and Joseph stories but also and especially in Psalm 118, the enthronement Psalm at the climax of Israel's Hallel cycle). The christological treasure here is subtly wrapped, but the parable of the Wicked Tenants starts to unwind it. Throughout this book, we will consider other examples that disclose still more of the hidden identity of Jesus.

How Do the Gospels Teach Us to Read the OT?

So far, I have done the easy part of my assignment, focusing on the ways in which the OT might teach us to read the Gospels. We turn now to the more difficult matter of *reading backwards*: How do the Gospels teach us to read the OT? Is such a project simply a category mistake, like talking about T. S. Eliot's influence on Shakespeare, or—worse—is it a hijacking of somebody else's scriptures? This time, I must confine myself to a single example, followed by some brief conclusions.

Luke 24:13-35: Opening the Scriptures. Let us consider Luke 24:13-35: Luke's account of the risen Jesus' encounter with two disciples on the road to Emmaus. In this episode, Luke highlights Jesus' role as exegete of the biblical story: the risen Lord becomes the definitive interpreter of "the things about himself in all the scriptures" (Luke 24:27).

Cleopas and his anonymous companion on the road to Emmaus are well acquainted with all the stories and traditions about Jesus' life, including the report of the empty tomb and the angelic proclamation of the resurrection (vv. 19-24), but they are nonetheless departing Jerusalem in a state of gloomy disappointment: "But we had hoped that he was the one to redeem Israel" (v. 21a). This is a moment of wrenching irony: Jesus, the redeemer of Israel, stands before them, yet they fail to recognize him.[21]

Jesus scolds them for their failure to believe *the prophets*[22] (interestingly, not for their failure to believe Jesus' own predictions of his death and resurrection) and begins to instruct them all over again: "Then beginning with Moses and all the prophets, he interpreted to them the things about himself in all the scriptures" (v. 27). As Walter Moberly has observed, the risen Jesus offers no new visions from heaven or mysteries from beyond the grave but instead focuses on the patient exposition of Israel's Scripture. The crucial truth lies there, not in some hidden heavenly revelation.[23] Furthermore, Luke's formulation suggests that testimony to Jesus is to be found "in all the Scriptures" (ἐν πάσαις ταῖς γραφαῖς), not just in a few isolated prooftexts. The whole story of Israel builds to its narrative climax in Jesus. That is what Jesus tries to teach them on the road.

It is essential to teach them about Scripture because Scripture forms the matrix within which the recent shattering events in Jerusalem become intelligible: "[A]s Jesus cannot be understood apart from Jewish scripture, Jewish scripture cannot be understood apart from Jesus; what is needed is an interpretation which relates the two—and it is this that Jesus provides (v. 27)."[24] Apart from this integrative interpretation, the puzzled Emmaus disciples have all the facts but lack the pattern that makes them meaningful. In other words, what is lacking is a figural interpretation of the Old Testament's psalms and stories. Luke's tantalizingly brief summary of the meaning-pattern is offered in verse 26: "Was it not necessary that the Messiah should suffer these things and then enter into his glory?" Somehow Jesus' exposition of Israel's Scripture will have to undertake the task of reading backwards: it will have to show *retrospectively* the pervasive presence of this theme—which had never been perceived by anyone in Israel prior to the crucifixion and resurrection.

Luke, as a skillful storyteller, does not yet give away all his secrets. He does not divulge the contents of this privileged exposition of the Bible by the risen Jesus. In order to see what Luke has in mind, we must await his second volume, where his accounts of the apostolic preaching draw heavily on scriptural texts.[25] Yet, strikingly, even Jesus' definitive peripatetic Bible study on the road to Emmaus does not produce understanding and recognition in the Emmaus disciples. (I will confess that this is some consolation to me as a teacher!) At least, Jesus' teaching does not produce that result immediately. The moment of recognition comes only as they sit at the table and Jesus breaks bread with them (vv. 30-32). This point, too, is significant for understanding how the Gospels teach us to read the OT. We come to understand Scripture only as we participate in the shared life of the community, enacted in meals shared at table.[26]

For those who participate in the practices of sharing modeled by Jesus, an "opening" occurs. It is not by accident that Luke uses this word twice in quick succession. When Jesus broke the bread and gave it to them, their eyes were *opened* (διηνοίχθησαν, v. 31) to recognize him; and as they recall his teaching, they say, "Weren't our hearts burning within us as he was speaking to us on the road, as he *opened* (διήνοιγεν) to us the Scriptures?" (v. 32). The disciples' faculties of perception are opened by God in such a way that they now not only recognize Jesus but also recognize the Scriptures to have been opened by Jesus' readings. The same word appears once more in the following account of Jesus' teaching of the disciples in Jerusalem: "Then he opened [διήνοιξεν] their minds to understand the scriptures" (v. 45). Reading the OT anew in light of the story of Jesus' death and resurrection opens both text and reader to new, previously unimagined, possibilities.

———

In conclusion, then, I offer once again a few summary remarks based on what we have learned from Luke 24. How do the Gospels teach us to read the OT?

(1) The Gospels teach us to read the OT for *figuration*. The literal historical sense of the OT is not denied or negated; rather, it becomes the vehicle for latent figural meanings unsuspected by the original author and readers. It points forward typologically to the gospel story. And, precisely because figural reading affirms the original historical reference of the text, it leaves open the possibility of respectful dialogue with other interpretations, other patterns of intertextual reception. This is a point of potentially great significance for conversation between Jews and Christians about the interpretation of Israel's Scripture.

(2) If we learn from the Gospel of Luke how to read the OT, we will see that the whole story of Israel builds to a narrative climax in the story of Jesus. In other words, we do not simply scour the OT for isolated

prooftexts and predictions; rather, we must perceive how the whole story of God's covenant promise unfolds and leads toward the events of Jesus' death and resurrection. For example, the saga of the exodus from bondage in Egypt and the pattern of Israel's exile and return become *prefigurations* of the Gospel.

(3) The figural disclosive reading that the Gospels teach occurs rightly in a community of discipleship and table fellowship. It is not an exercise that can be confined to libraries and lecture halls; it draws us to become participants in the story that we read and narrate anew.

Thus, we have begun to see some of the ways in which the OT and Gospels interact and interpret one another: in the new situation created by the death and resurrection of Jesus, Israel's Scripture is to be comprehensively construed as a witness to the gospel. This claim is not merely an ancient hermeneutical mistake that Christians can now decide to abandon; it is integral to the Gospels' witness about the identity of Jesus. According to these Gospel texts, those who fail to read the OT this way have not yet fully understood it, for understanding is rendered possible only after the encounter with the risen Jesus. At the same time, though, the resurrection of Jesus will remain a mute, uninterpretable puzzle unless it is placed firmly within the OT's story of Israel. The disciples on the way to Emmaus had already heard it reported that Jesus was alive, but *because they did not know how to locate this report within Israel's story*, it seemed a curious and meaningless claim. Their incomprehension—which prefigures the interpretive helplessness of late modern readers—exemplifies the grimly ironic dictum with which Luke's parable of the Rich Man and Lazarus concludes: "'If they do not listen to Moses and the prophets, neither will they be convinced even if someone rises from the dead'" (Luke 16:31). That is our plight today. And I speak not only of a post-Christian pluralistic culture that does not know the Scriptures. I speak also of the church. For much of the church today, Moses and the prophets belong to a closed and unknown book. The good news of Luke 24, however, is that the story does not end in incomprehension and hermeneutical failure because the one who rose from the dead teaches us anew how to read backwards—and therefore how to listen to Moses and the prophets.

2

FIGURING THE MYSTERY
Reading Scripture with Mark

"Let the Reader Understand."

The Gospel of Mark tells a mysterious story enveloped in apocalyptic urgency, a story that focuses relentlessly on the cross and ends on a note of hushed, enigmatic hope. Many of the key images in this mysterious narrative are drawn from Israel's Scriptures; indeed, a reader who fails to discern the significance of these images can hardly grasp Mark's message.

But Mark's way of drawing upon Scripture, like his narrative style more generally, is indirect and allusive. Mark for the most part works his narrative magic through hints and allusions, giving just enough clues to tease the reader into further exploration and reflection. On rare occasions, he steps from behind the curtain to call the reader's attention to a particularly important intertextual allusion (e.g., "Let the reader understand" in 13:14), but for the most part his scriptural references are woven seamlessly into the fabric of the story. The story is intelligible, at one level, for readers who do not hear the scriptural echoes. But for those who do have ears to hear, new levels of complexity and significance open up.

To cite an obvious example, Mark tells the story of Jesus' entry to Jerusalem riding on a colt without any authorial comment whatever about scriptural fulfillment (11:1-11). But the reader who perceives the subliminal symbolism of Zechariah 9:9 imbedded in the action will more fully grasp the significance of the episode. In this case, readers who lack the requisite encyclopedia of reception to "get" the allusion are helped out by one of Mark's earliest readers, Matthew, who eagerly supplies the

quotation of Zechariah, along with an explanatory reassurance that this
event took place in order to fulfill what was written by the prophet (Matt
21:4-5).[1] But this example is merely the tip of an iceberg of intertextual
allusion in Mark; we would be singularly inept readers if we confined our
recognition of these intertexts, and their significance, to the few cases that
Matthew has happened to elucidate.

My remarks will be divided into two parts: I will first explore a few
passages in which Mark draws allusively on Scripture to shape his narration of the identity of Jesus, and then I will step back for some broader
reflection on Mark's distinctive hermeneutical strategy for interpreting
Israel's sacred texts.

How Does Mark Use Scripture to Narrate
the Identity of Jesus?

Mark's carefully layered plot gradually elaborates the mystery surrounding the identity of Jesus. In the early chapters of the story, he is a powerful, wonder-working figure who seems comparable to Elijah or one of the
prophets of old (6:15). At various points in the tale, his words and actions
seem to correspond typologically to the words and actions of Moses or
Jeremiah. And as the plot moves toward its climax in Jerusalem, there are
abundant hints that Jesus is the bearer of David's legacy as king of Israel.
Each of these accounts of Jesus' identity illumines some facet of his mission and identity, yet they all remain tentative, partial, and inadequate.
Jesus remains elusive and avoids direct speech about the secret of his own
personhood, except in his cryptic utterances about the Son of Man.

The revelatory declaration in Mark 14:62, the capstone of these Son of
Man sayings, seems to divulge the secret at last.

> Again the high priest asked him, "Are you the Messiah, the Son of the
> Blessed One?" Jesus said, "I am; and 'you will see the Son of Man seated
> at the right hand of the Power,' and 'coming with the clouds of heaven.'"
> (14:61-62)

After so much evasion and deferral, at last Jesus unambiguously declares
that he is "the Messiah, the Son of the Blessed One" and that he will
ascend to heavenly eschatological dignity as the Son of Man, exercising
dominion over the world, as prefigured in Daniel 7:13-14:

I saw in the night visions, and behold, with the clouds of heaven there came one like a son of man, and he came to the Ancient of Days and was presented before him. And to him was given dominion and glory and kingdom, that all peoples, nations, and languages should serve him; his dominion is an everlasting dominion, which shall not pass away, and his kingdom one that shall not be destroyed. (RSV)

This astounding claim explains much that has gone before. If Jesus is ultimately to rule alongside God, we now understand more fully, for example, how he can presume to reinterpret Torah with sovereign freedom (e.g., Mark 2:23-28: ". . . the Son of Man is lord even of the sabbath"; cf. 7:1-23). We can understand the mysterious event of the transfiguration (9:2-8) as a prefiguration of Jesus' ultimate heavenly glory. We can understand why it is not sufficient to interpret Jesus as a great prophet or even as the expected Davidic king, for he is one who is still greater. The categories of prophet and messiah are not wrong, but they fail to do full justice to his identity.

Yet even the title "Son of Man," understood in its full Danielic context, does not exhaust the mystery. Mark's characterization of Jesus is still more complex and elusive, and there are several hints scattered through the story that lead us to press the inquiry forward. If Jesus is identified, through Mark's references to Daniel 7, as the eschatological Son of Man enthroned in heavenly glory, the question inevitably arises of how to understand his relation to the "Ancient of Days," the God of Israel. If Israel's God is a jealous God who brooks no other gods before his face (Exod 20:1-3; Deut 5:6-7), who then is this figure who exercises everlasting dominion, with whom the heavenly throne room is to be shared?[2] In light of Jesus' breathtaking self-disclosure in the trial scene (14:62), we are compelled to reread the whole story to see whether there are further clues to Jesus' identity that we might have missed along the way.

And upon rereading, we discover numerous passages scattered through this Gospel that offer intimations of a disturbing truth: *Jesus' identity with the one God of Israel.* Unlike the Gospel of John—which explicitly declares that Jesus is the *Logos,* the Son who is one with the Father—Mark shies away from overt ontological declarations. Nonetheless, Mark's Gospel suggests that Jesus is, in some way that defies comprehension, the embodiment of God's presence.[3] Mark never quite dares to articulate this claim explicitly; it is too scandalous for direct speech. For Mark, the character of God's presence in Jesus is a mystery that can be approached only by indirection, through riddle-like allusions to the OT. Let us, then, consider several passages in which the riddle is posed.

Mark 1:2-3: Who is the Kyrios? Mark's opening mixed citation already contains a major clue about the divine identity of Jesus. Mark weaves together citations of Malachi 3:1, Exodus 23:20, and Isaiah 40:3 to portray John the baptizer as the messenger sent by God as a harbinger of the new exodus and the restoration of Israel. John's message prepares the way for "one who is more powerful" who is soon to come (Mark 1:7-8). Who is that more powerful one? His mysterious identity is strongly suggested by the Isaian language that Mark cites: "Prepare the way of *the Lord* [κυρίου], make his paths straight" (Mark 1:3b, quoting Isa 40:3).

In Isaiah 40, there can be no question that "the Lord" is the LORD God of Israel in the Hebrew text, (יהוה), who will return to Zion to set things right, and "the way of the LORD" refers to the path that God will make through the desert, leading the triumphant procession of returning exiles. The full citation from Isaiah 40:3 reads, "In the wilderness prepare the way of the LORD, make straight in the desert a highway *for our God.*" The emphasis in Isaiah's prophetic vision lies on "the return of Yahweh's actual presence" as the cause of deliverance.[4] This is made abundantly clear a few verses later:

> Get you up to a high mountain,
> O Zion, herald of good tidings;
> lift up your voice with strength,
> O Jerusalem, herald of good tidings,
> lift it up, do not fear;
> say to the cities of Judah,
> "*Here is your God!*"
> *See, the Lord GOD* [κύριος] *comes with might,*
> and his arm rules for him;
> his reward is with him,
> and his recompense before him. (Isa 40:9-10)

Two points, then, are unmistakably clear: Isaiah 40 prophesies the coming of the *Kyrios* (the Lord God) to reign, and Mark appropriates this prophecy to characterize John's preparation of the way for the coming of *Jesus.* The only question is whether we should draw the obvious inference that, for Mark, Jesus is in fact to be identified with the *Kyrios* of whom Isaiah speaks.[5]

If Mark's citation of Isaiah 40 carries forward the substance of its original sense,[6] there is an implicit claim about Jesus' divine status in the opening lines of this Gospel.[7]

It would be hasty to conclude on the basis of this one citation that Mark unequivocally identifies Jesus with the *Kyrios* of the Old Testament. Yet we would be heedless readers indeed if we failed to wonder why Mark selects Isaiah 40:3 as the keynote of his account of Jesus' activity. A certain ambiguity hovers about these opening verses of Mark's story. Should we see in Jesus' arrival on the scene the veiled but palpable fulfillment of Isaiah's fervent expectation?

Mark 2:7: Who can forgive sins but God alone? The next passage that contains a clue about Jesus' divine identity is the story of the healing of the paralytic (2:1-12), the first unit of Mark's opening cycle of controversy discourses (2:1–3:6). In this form-critically complex story,[8] Jesus not only performs a dramatic healing but also asserts his authority to forgive sins. Here there is no explicit OT citation, but the question of the skeptical scribes sends out ripples of significance when it is read against the background of the OT: "Why does this fellow speak in this way? It is blasphemy! Who can forgive sins but God alone?"[9]

In Israel's Scripture, as the scribes' incredulous protest implies, it is beyond doubt that the prerogative to forgive sins belongs to God alone. Since sin is offense against God, only God has the right to declare it cancelled. Several key passages may come to mind as the basis for the scribes' question, particularly Exodus 34:6-7, in which God, appearing to Moses on Mount Sinai on the occasion of the giving of the second set of tablets of the Law, solemnly proclaims an account of his own identity in which forgiveness of sins plays a constitutive part:

> "The LORD, the LORD,
> a God merciful and gracious,
> slow to anger, and abounding in steadfast love and faithfulness,
> keeping steadfast love for the thousandth generation,
> *forgiving iniquity and transgression and sin,*
> yet by no means clearing the guilty,
> but visiting the iniquity of the parents
> upon the children
> and the children's children,
> to the third and the fourth generation."

This central confession of Israel's faith posits forgiveness of sins as belonging to God's character. Similarly, the scribes in Mark 2 might be recalling Isaiah 43:25: "I, I am He who blots out your transgressions for my own sake, and I will not remember your sins."[10]

Jesus' response to the scribes' thoroughly understandable objection is to command the paralytic to stand up and walk, as a visible sign of his own authority as Son of Man to forgive sins on earth (Mark 2:8-11). And here the reference to the authority of the Son of Man foreshadows Mark's later explicit evocation of Daniel 7, with its emphasis on the Son of Man's dominion over the whole earth.[11]

With regard to the question of Jesus' identity, however, the scribes' question lingers. Who can forgive sins but God alone? One might read 2:10 to mean that Jesus, as Son of Man, is exercising on earth a delegated authority from God to forgive sins,[12] but in light of the already noted identification of Jesus as the *Kyrios* (1:3), the reader of Mark's Gospel may ponder at least the possibility that his sovereign authority to forgive sins is not just delegated.

Mark 4:35-41: Who then is this, that even the wind and sea obey him? If the first two chapters of Mark have kindled sparks of insight into his divine identity, the rising wind of Mark 4:35-41 fans the sparks into a fire. In the story of the stilling of the storm, after Jesus rebukes the wind and orders the sea to be still, he scolds the disciples for their lack of faith. For their part, they ask each other, in awe, "Who then is this, that even the wind and the sea obey him?"

Mark provocatively leaves the question unanswered. The words hang suspended over the story—leaving the reader to supply the answer. For any reader versed in Israel's Scripture, there can be only one possible answer: it is the Lord God of Israel who has the power to command wind and sea and to subdue the chaotic forces of nature. Resonating in the background of Mark's story of Jesus' calming the sea is a vivid passage from Psalm 107:

> Some went down to the sea in ships,
> doing business on the mighty waters;
> they saw the deeds of the LORD,
> his wondrous works in the deep.
> For he commanded and raised the stormy wind,
> which lifted up the waves of the sea.

They mounted up to heaven, they went down to the depths;
their courage melted away in their calamity [cf. Mark 4:40];
they reeled and staggered like drunkards,
and were at their wits' end.
Then they cried to the LORD in their trouble,
and he brought them out from their distress;
he made the storm be still,
and the waves of the sea were hushed. (107:23-32; cf. Mark 4:39)

What then are we to conclude about the identity of Jesus, since his role in the story is precisely the role ascribed to the LORD in Psalm 107?[13] Jesus' mastery over the wind and waves demonstrates that he is the possessor of a power that the OT consistently assigns to the LORD God alone. It is God who rebuked the waters and formed the dry land, God who parted the sea for Israel, God who made the storm be still. Well might the disciples ask, "Who then is this . . . ?"

Mark 6:34: Who is the shepherd of Israel? In the opening lines of Mark's story of the miraculous feeding of the five thousand (6:30-44), we are told that when he saw the great crowd of people, "he had compassion for them, because they were like sheep without a shepherd; and he began to teach them many things."[14] In light of Mark's insistent suggestions about the divine identity of Jesus, the image of "sheep without a shepherd" evokes a significant intertextual echo from Ezekiel's poignant portrayal of the scattered flock of Israel. In Ezekiel 34, the description of David as the shepherd/king over Israel (vv. 23-24) is secondary to a more fundamental prophecy about the agency whereby the sheep are to be rescued:

> For thus says the Lord GOD: I myself will search for my sheep, and will seek them out. As shepherds seek out their flocks when they are among their scattered sheep, so I will seek out my sheep. I will rescue them from all the places to which they have been scattered on a day of clouds and thick darkness. I will bring them out from the peoples and gather them from the countries, and will bring them into their own land; . . . I myself will be the shepherd of my sheep, and I will make them lie down, says the Lord GOD. (Ezek 34:11-15)

Significantly, the LXX adds at the end of verse 15 the phrase καὶ γνώσονται ὅτι ἐγώ εἰμι κύριος ("and they shall know that I am the LORD"). The true shepherd in Ezekiel's prophecy—whose identity is revealed through his act of feeding the sheep—is the LORD God himself.

What, then, shall we infer when Mark tells us that Jesus sees the people as sheep without a shepherd and then makes them sit down on the green grass and feeds them? If the next story, the story of Jesus walking on the sea, is to be connected closely with the miraculous feeding, it may offer a hint of how such questions are to be answered.

Mark 6:45-52: Who walks on the sea? In Mark 6, we encounter another strange epiphany during a sea-crossing: Jesus comes to the disciples walking on the sea. In response to their terror, he offers a word of reassurance: θαρσεῖτε, ἐγώ εἰμι· μὴ φοβεῖσθε ("Take heart, it is I; do not be afraid"). Should we read this as another revelatory disclosure of Jesus' divine identity?

There is no OT citation in this story, and the image of God's walking on the sea is not so widely attested as the image of his commanding and stilling the waves. Commentators seeking to highlight exodus typology in Mark's story sometimes cite passages such as Psalm 77:19, Isaiah 43:16, and Isaiah 51:9-10,[15] but these are not really apposite, for they refer to the exodus sea-crossing in which God parted the waters to lead the people through *on dry ground* (Exod 14:21-22; 15:19). The image in these passages is not one of the deity walking *atop* the waters of the sea. There is, however, at least one OT passage that paints a picture prefiguring Mark's sea-walking story: a doxological passage in Job, portraying God as sovereign over all creation, acclaims him as the one "who alone stretched out the heavens and trampled the waves of the Sea" (Job 9:8). In its original context, this was probably meant as a reference to God's subduing the primordial watery chaos, but the LXX offers a rendering of Job 9:8 that may be of considerable importance for understanding Mark 6:45-52: ὁ τανύσας τὸν οὐρανὸν μόνος καὶ περιπατῶν ὡς ἐπ* ἐδάφους ἐπὶ θαλάσσης ("who alone stretched out heaven *and walks upon the sea as upon dry ground*").[16]

If Mark had Job 9 in mind, it would help to explain another notoriously puzzling feature of the water-walking tale. In Mark's telling of the story, when Jesus comes walking on the sea, the narrator comments cryptically, "He intended to pass them by" (ἤθελεν παρελθεῖν αὐτούς [6:48]). This remark has consistently baffled interpreters (beginning with the evangelist Matthew, who deletes the clause [Matt 14:25]) and generated labored explanations, such as Augustine's suggestion that "his intent in passing by them was to serve the purpose of eliciting those outcries in response to which he would then come to bring relief."[17] (This explanation is particularly unsatisfactory because according to the story the disciples do not cry out to Jesus for help; they are terrified of him because they think he is a ghost.) If we recognize the allusion to Job 9, however, we may glimpse a far more illuminating reading. In the same passage that speaks of the Creator God walking upon the sea, Job goes on to marvel at the way in which God eludes his own limited understanding:

> He is wise in heart, and mighty in strength
> —who has resisted him, and succeeded?—
> he who removes mountains, and they do not know it,
> when he overturns them in his anger;
> who shakes the earth out of its place,
> and its pillars tremble;
> who commands the sun, and it does not rise;
> who seals up the stars;
> who alone stretched out the heavens
> and trampled the waves of the Sea [LXX: καὶ περιπατῶν ὡς ἐπ᾽ ἐδάφους
> ἐπὶ θαλάσσης ("and walks upon the sea as upon dry ground")];
> who made the Bear and Orion,
> the Pleiades and the chambers of the south;
> who does great things beyond understanding,
> and marvelous things without number.
> *Look, he passes by me, and I do not see him;*
> *he moves on* [LXX: παρέλθῃ με, "he passes me by"], *but I do not perceive*
> *him.* (Job 9:4-11)[18]

Thus, in Job 9 the image of God's walking on the sea is linked with a confession of God's mysterious transcendence of human comprehension: God's "passing by" is a metaphor for our inability to grasp his power.[19] This metaphor accords deeply with Mark's emphasis on the elusiveness of the divine presence in Jesus. Thus, the story of Jesus' epiphanic walking on the sea, read against the background of Job 9, can be perceived as the signature image of Markan Christology.

To these observations should be added the insight that the verb παρελθεῖν almost surely alludes to Exodus 33:17-23 and 34:6, where God is said to "pass by" Moses in order to reveal his glory indirectly, for "no one shall see me and live."[20] The LXX repeatedly uses παρελθεῖν in this passage, with the result that it subsequently becomes "almost a technical term for a divine epiphany."[21] Thus, Mark's mysterious statement in Mark

6:48, read as an allusion to the Exodus theophany, suggests simultaneously that Jesus' walking on the water is a manifestation of divine glory and that it remains indirect and beyond full comprehension—as the disciples' uncomprehending response amply demonstrates (6:51-52).

In this narrative context, there is little doubt that we should also hear Jesus' comforting address to the disciples ("It is I [ἐγώ εἰμι]; do not be afraid" [6:50]) as an echo of the self-revelatory speech of the God of Abraham, of Isaac, and of Jacob speaking from the burning bush in Exodus 3:14: "I AM WHO I AM" (LXX: ἐγώ εἰμι ὁ ὤν).[22] Thus, when Jesus speaks this same phrase, "I am," in his sea-crossing epiphany, it serves to underscore the claim of divine identity that is implicitly present in the story as a whole.

The obtuse disciples, who have failed to grasp the meaning of the miracle of the loaves, fail also to understand even a sign so dramatic as this one. Matthew, finding their dullness inexplicable, writes a different ending to the story: in Matthew, when Jesus gets into the boat, the disciples promptly worship him and declare, "Truly you are the Son of God" (Matt 14:33). In this way, they model the response to Jesus that Matthew seeks to encourage in the church.[23] Mark, I would suggest, seeks to elicit a response of a slightly different kind: those who have picked up the clues Mark has offered will perceive that God is strangely present in Jesus, but their response—at least at this point in the story—will be one of reverent reticence. By refusing to trumpet the secret of Jesus' identity, instead signifying it through mysterious symbol-laden narrative, Mark is teaching his readers to wonder and to listen more deeply before they start talking about things too wonderful for their understanding.

Once we observe Mark's pattern of hinting that Jesus is the mysteriously embodied presence of Israel's God, we might approach other texts in this Gospel with fresh eyes, particularly two of Mark's notorious "riddle" texts. In one of these, Jesus replies to an inquirer who has addressed him as "Good Teacher" by asking provocatively, "Why do you call me 'good'? No one is good except one, God" (Mark 10:18). And in the cycle of controversy discourses in the Temple in Mark 12, Jesus poses a vexing riddle for the scribes: in Psalm 110, David refers to his eschatologically triumphant heir as *Kyrios*; so how can he be David's son? In neither case does Mark offer the reader an answer to the riddles that Jesus poses. But I would suggest that the key to finding an answer lies in the clues we have already encountered earlier in the narrative, clues that point to Jesus as the embodied presence of the one confessed in Israel's *Shema* and praised as *Kyrios* in Israel's Psalter.

Complicating the picture: Jesus' non-identity with God? Alongside the passages we have surveyed, we must acknowledge that several passages in Mark's Gospel seem to distinguish Jesus from Israel's God. We need not discuss each instance in detail; a cursory overview of the evidence suffices to show that Mark's narrative does not posit a simple undifferentiated equivalence between Jesus and the God of Israel: even in his eschatological exaltation, Jesus the Son of Man will be summoned to sit *at the right hand* of the throne of God (12:35-37; 14:62). This is a position of extraordinary honor and power, to be sure, but is exalted proximity quite the same thing as simple *identity* with the God of Israel? Jesus declares his own ignorance about the time of the end, in contrast to the knowledge of the Father (13:32). Indeed, several passages identify Jesus as the "Son" (1:11; 9:7; 12:6) and distinguish his role from that of the Father (8:38; 11:25; 14:36). This Father/Son language binds Jesus in the closest possible relationship with God, whose glory and authority Jesus shares, while maintaining some distinction of roles and persons. This relationship is perhaps most clearly expressed in Jesus' prayer in Gethsemane, in which he subordinates himself to the will of the Father: "Abba, Father, for you all things are possible; remove this cup from me; yet, not what I want, but what you want" (14:36). Here, Jesus seems to play the role of Israel rather than the role of God: in the midst of doubt and agony, he submits and becomes obedient.[24] Finally, the cry of dereliction from the cross once again draws on the language of the Psalms to express not only a distinction between Jesus and God but also a stark separation: "My God, my God, why have you forsaken me?" (Mark 15:34, echoing Ps 22:1).[25]

In light of these elements of Mark's story, how are we to understand the pervasive Markan indicators that Jesus is mysteriously the embodiment of God's presence? Mark offers us no conceptual solution to the problem. Rather, his narrative holds these elements in taut suspension.[26] His central character, Jesus, seems to be at the same time—if we may put it crudely—both the God of Israel and a human being not simply identical with the God of Israel. Thus, Mark's story already poses the riddles that the church's theologians later sought to solve in the christological controversies of the fourth and fifth centuries. The logical tensions are internal to Mark's account; they are not created only when we set the "divine" Jesus of the Fourth Gospel in contrast to the "human" Jesus of the Synoptics. (This caricature is misleading in both its terms.) Rather, Mark's story repeatedly draws upon OT imagery to portray the human Jesus as the Lord whom wind and sea obey.

Hidden in Order to Be Revealed: Mark's Scriptural Hermeneutics

One implication of the foregoing analysis is this: if the scriptural inter-texts in Mark are ignored, a diminished Christology inevitably follows.[27] The full impact of Mark's Christology can be discerned only when we attend to *the poetics of allusion* imbedded in Mark's intertextual narrative strategy.

One way of putting my point about Mark's use of Scripture is to say that his hermeneutical strategy for reading Israel's sacred texts is anal-ogous to his understanding of the function of parables, as disclosed in Jesus' answer to the disciples' question about his enigmatic manner of teaching in parables. Jesus' reply speaks of a "mystery of the kingdom of God" that is disclosed to some but hidden from others in the form of parables (4:11-12). Yet at the end of Mark's parable chapter, we find this authorial comment: "And with many such parables, he spoke to them the word, *just as they were able to hear.* He did not speak to them apart from a parable, but privately to his own disciples he explained all things" (4:33-34). There appears to be some tension between verses 11-12 and verse 33. In the former, the parables seem to have the function of *hiding* the message of the kingdom, but in the latter, they seem to be instruments of communication that allow Jesus' listeners to grasp the message at their own level of understanding. Is this an outright contradiction, a sign of Mark's incompetence and inconsistency as a storyteller? Might it be a redactional seam, betraying the presence of different sources? Or, on the other hand, does it communicate something essential about the charac-ter of the paradoxical veiled communication we find both in the parables and in the identity of Jesus himself throughout this Gospel?

Mark himself gives us a clue to the answer in a densely packed para-graph lodged in the midst of Jesus' parable discourse:

And he said to them, "The lamp doesn't come, does it, to be placed under a bushel-basket or under the bed? Does it not come in order to placed on a lampstand? For there is not anything that is hidden except in order to be revealed, nor is anything secret except in order to be disclosed. If anyone has ears to hear, let him hear." And he said to them, "Watch what you hear! The measure with which you measure will be measured back to you, and still more will be added to you. Whoever has, it will be given to him; and as for the one who does not have, even what he has will be taken away from him." (4:21-25)

In its context in Mark 4, as a direct continuation of Jesus' answer about teaching in parables, this is surely to be understood as a figurative discourse about the hermeneutics of hearing and understanding the word.

A comparison of Mark 4:22 to the parallels in Matthew 10:26 and Luke 8:17 reveals an interesting difference. The saying in its Matthean and Lukan forms draws a contrast between present concealment and *future* revelation.

Matthew: "For nothing is veiled that will not be revealed, and nothing is hidden that will not be known."

Luke: "For there is nothing hidden that will not be disclosed, nor is anything secret that will not be known."

But Mark's form of the saying highlights the intentionality of the hiding:

Mark: "For there is not anything that is hidden except *in order to* [ἵνα] be revealed, nor is anything secret except *in order to* [ἵνα] be disclosed."[28]

The hiddenness somehow belongs to the revelatory purpose or even promotes the revelation.

In view of all we have seen in Mark's Gospel, it would not be too much to suggest that the purpose implied here is the divine purpose to offer veiled self-revelation in the person of Jesus, whose identity is finally fully disclosed only at the moment of greatest obscurity, his shameful death on a cross ("Truly this man was the Son of God").

The suggestion that Mark 4:21-22 speaks in a veiled manner of divine self-disclosure is also supported by the odd construction of the saying in 4:21, literally, "Does the lamp *come* [ἔρχεται] . . . ?" English translators characteristically find this formulation intolerable and render it with a passive voice construction of some different verb, such as "Is a lamp *brought* . . . ?" (NRSV).[29] But in fact, the sentence as Mark wrote it describes the lamp as an active agent that "comes." The nearly inescapable consequence of this observation is that Mark has shaped this saying as a christological parable about Jesus' coming into the world.[30] When it is joined to the paradoxical saying in verse 22 about things hidden in order to be revealed, we are close to the heart of Mark's Christology and, I would suggest, his hermeneutical approach to Israel's Scripture.

That is why the very next verses contain an urgent exhortation to listen carefully: "Pay careful attention to what you hear," says Jesus, "because if you 'measure' generously in interpreting the word, still more rewards will follow. But if you are a stingy hearer who hears only the literal surface sense, your reading of the Gospel—and of Israel's Scripture—will offer only diminishing returns, leading finally to nothing but impoverishment."

That is of course a broad paraphrase of Mark 4:23-25, but contextually in Mark 4 we are compelled to understand verses 24-25 as a teaching about how to hear the proclaimed word. Mark has shaped these sayings, which may have been in the earlier tradition a scattered group of logia,[31] into a cohesive exhortation about hermeneutics. Readers are called to listen closely to what might be hidden in the text in order to enter fully into the outpouring of signification that awaits the attentive interpreter.

Mark's hermeneutical directive, however uncongenial for modernist interpreters accustomed to seek a single clear and explicit "original sense" in texts, is in fact precisely attuned to the way that figurative language actually works—including the metaphorical discourse characteristic of apocalyptic texts. Metaphors do not deal in direct statement; rather, they intensify meaning precisely by concealing it, by speaking in an indirect mode and saying something other than what is meant. Robert Frost phrased this insight simply: "Poetry provides the one permissible way of saying one thing and meaning another."[32] And the literary critic Frank Kermode, in his penetrating study of the hermeneutics of Mark's Gospel, observed, "Parable, it seems, may proclaim a truth as a herald does, and at the same time conceal truth like an oracle."[33]

In light of these observations, the importance of Mark 4:21-25 as a hermeneutical directive for the Gospel as a whole can hardly be overstated. Mark is alerting his readers that christological signification may be hidden but that attentive listening can discern, within the Gospel's parabolic figuration, layers of meaning that point to "the mystery of the kingdom of God." It is no accident that in 4:11 Mark writes the singular noun μυστήριον, rather than the plural μυστήρια, which occurs in the synoptic parallels (Matt 13:11 and Luke 8:10). For Mark, the *singular* mystery disclosed in and through the narrative is nothing other than the identity of Jesus himself, the Crucified Messiah who is also paradoxically the embodiment of the God of Israel.

And yet to state this claim bluntly in so many words, as I have just done, is to betray Mark's far more circumspect way of communicating the mystery. It is to blurt out crassly a secret so huge that its right expression must be concealed in figures, riddles, and whispers. In a discussion of Mark's trial narrative, Rowan Williams gets the delicate balance just right, in a way sympathetically responsive to Mark's manner of telling the story:

> Throughout [Mark's] Gospel, Jesus holds back from revealing who he is because, it seems, he cannot believe that there are words that will tell the truth about him in the mouths of others. What will be said of him is bound to be untrue—that he is master of all circumstances; that he can heal where he wills; that he is the expected triumphant deliverer, the Anointed. . . . "There is a kind of truth which, when it is said, becomes untrue." Remember, the world Mark depicts is not a reasonable one; it is full of demons and suffering and abused power. How, in such a world, *could* there be a language in which it could truly be said who Jesus is?[34]

But Mark is not reduced to simple silence. "How, in such a world, *could* there be a language in which it could truly be said who Jesus is?" Mark's answer is that there *is* such a language in the stories and symbols of Israel's Scripture, read in counterpoint with the stories about Jesus. If it is misleading, or careless of the mystery, to state flatly, "Jesus is the God of Israel"—just as it is not permitted to speak the ineffable name of God figured in the Tetragrammaton—there is still a way of *narrating* who Jesus is by telling stories in which he has the authority to forgive sins, to still storms, to walk on the sea, to feed the scattered sheep as the true shepherd, to make the deaf to hear and the mute to speak. There is a way to narrate who Jesus is by identifying John the Baptist as the voice in the wilderness who will proclaim Isaiah's gospel message of the end of exile by crying, "Prepare the way of the *Kyrios*." Through the poetics of allusion, Mark gestures toward the astounding truth. Those who have ears to hear will hear.

Even such indirect confessional claims, however, must be read within the larger context of Mark's story. The identity of Jesus as the mysterious embodiment of Israel's God can never be separated from his identity as the Crucified One. And therein lies a still deeper layer of the mystery: If Jesus is the embodiment of Israel's God, and if the body in whom these figural correspondences to Israel's Scripture are enacted ends up nailed to a cross, what does that tell us about the identity of God?

Has Mark thought through such implications of his way of telling the story? We cannot say, because he does not say. But readers who listen carefully to the resonances of Israel's Scripture in Mark's Gospel and then see how the story drives toward the passion narrative may find themselves, like the women in Mark's artful dramatic ending, reduced, at least for a time, to silence: "They said nothing to anyone, for they were afraid" (Mark 16:8). The fear of the women is, of course, a response to the message of the resurrection of Jesus the Crucified One. I would suggest that a similar response of reticent fear and trembling is equally appropriate when we read the story of the crucifixion, if we have rightly followed Mark's narrative clues about the identity of the one on the cross.

So, if we seek to read Scripture through Mark's eyes, what will we find? We will find ourselves drawn into the contemplation of a paradoxical revelation that shatters our categories and exceeds our understanding. We will learn to stand before the mystery in silence, to acknowledge the limitation of our understanding, and to wonder. The "meaning" of Mark's portrayal of the identity of Jesus cannot be rightly stated in flat propositional language; instead, it can be disclosed only gradually in the form of narrative, through hints and allusions that project the story of Jesus onto the background of Israel's story. As Mark superimposes the two stories on one another, remarkable new patterns emerge, patterns that lead us into a truth too overwhelming to be approached in any other way.

This reading of Mark as scriptural interpreter corresponds closely to an important stream of interpretation of Mark's Gospel in the Orthodox tradition. On the annual feast day of St. Mark the Evangelist, there is a prayer in the Greek Orthodox liturgy that invites the congregation to give honor to Mark for his distinctive, mysterious way of bearing witness: "Come, let us praise Mark, the herald of the heavenly mystagogy [τῆς οὐρανίου μυσταγωγίας τὸν κήρυκα], and the proclaimer of the gospel."[35] *Herald of the heavenly mystagogy*—that is, one who proclaims a message that leads us into the mystery. Our study of Mark suggests that Mark's proclamatory mystagogy is meant to lead readers, through a mysteriously allusive reading of Israel's Scripture, into recognizing Jesus as the embodiment of the God of Israel.

3

Torah Transfigured

Reading Scripture with Matthew

Matthew as Reader of Scripture

In the opening chapter of *The Wound of Knowledge*, Rowan Williams writes: "Christian faith has its beginnings in an experience of profound contradictoriness, an experience which so questioned the religious categories of its time that the resulting reorganization of religious language was a centuries-long task."[1] The "experience of profound contradictoriness" is, of course, the crucifixion of Jesus as the event that somehow brought God's salvation to the world: "the paradox of God's purpose made flesh in a dead and condemned man."[2] The "reorganization of religious language" to which Williams refers is the subsequent process of *retrospective reinterpretation* of Israel's traditions and of the earliest stories about Jesus, in dialogue with one another, and in light of the events of the cross and resurrection. It is, in other words, a process of *reading backwards* in light of new revelatory events. We see the beginnings of this "reorganization" within the NT itself in the NT writers' reinterpretations of Israel's Scripture.

I suggested in the previous chapter that the Gospel of Mark reads Scripture in an indirect, allusive fashion that leads the reader into meditation on the mystery of the relation between Jesus and the God of Israel. Indeed, as we encounter Mark's readings of Scripture, we are reminded of Williams' further comment about the difficulty and cost of encountering God's self-disclosure: "The greatness of the great Christian saints lies in their readiness to be questioned, judged, stripped naked and left speechless by that which lies at the center of their faith."[3] From this point of view, we can perhaps better understand the speechlessness with which Mark's

Gospel astonishingly ends: "They said nothing to anyone, for they were afraid" (Mark 16:8). Mark bears witness to an early stage in the reorganization of Israel's religious language; his indirection and reticence attest the enormity of the claims he is making about Jesus' identity,[4] as well as the reverent caution with which his community of readers might rightly receive such claims.

We turn now to consider the way in which the Gospel of Matthew advances the task of reorganizing Israel's religious language. What sort of a reader of Scripture is Matthew? Although Matthew builds on the foundation laid by Mark's Gospel, he shows little of Mark's restraint in pressing narrative claims about Jesus and linking them to Old Testament texts. Matthew is far more overt than Mark in his interpretative strategies; indeed, in many passages we find him providing explicit explanations of Mark's hints and allusions.

For example, Matthew's renarration of Jesus' apocalyptic discourse closely follows the script given by Mark, in which Jesus refers to a mysterious sign that should warn his followers to flee the city: "But when you see the abomination of desolation set up where it ought not to be (let the reader understand), then those in Judea must flee to the mountains" (Mark 13:14). As we have noted, this is one of the few places where Mark winks knowingly at the reader, signaling the presence of an allusion and trusting the reader to take the hint. Matthew repeats the saying, but he wants to make sure that the reader *will* understand, and so he glosses the text with additional information: "But when you see the abomination of desolation—*the one spoken of by the prophet Daniel*—standing *in the holy place* (let the reader understand), then those in Judea must flee to the mountains" (Matt 24:15). Ever the careful scribe, Matthew has specified the textual source for the reader who may need to look it up. He has also clarified the indefinite location of the event—not just "where it ought not to be," but specifically "in the holy place" (i.e., the Temple). In instances like this, it is as though Matthew is producing an annotated study Bible, providing notes and references that will give the uninitiated reader enough information to perform the necessary interpretation. Paul Minear has described this Gospel, in studied paradox, as a "training manual for prophets."[5]

Matthew has organized his material in a didactic, user-friendly fashion, making it unmistakably explicit that Jesus is the fulfillment of Israel's

Scriptures. It is therefore not without reason that when the fourfold
Gospel canon was later assembled, Matthew was placed first.[6] Nor was
it without reason that Matthew became the Gospel most frequently cited
by early Christian writers and that commentaries were written on it by
Origen, Jerome, John Chrysostom, Theodore of Mopsuestia, and Cyril of
Alexandria, to mention just some of the patristic authors who focused on
this Gospel.[7] (On the other hand, we have virtually no patristic commentaries on Mark.) Matthew successfully organized the Jesus tradition in a
form that made it clear, harmonious, and accessible.

When we consider Matthew's use of the OT, the first thing that springs
to mind is his distinctive manner of introducing prooftexts through a
repeated formula in which the Evangelist addresses the reader directly
in an authorial voiceover: "This took place to fulfill what had been spoken through the prophet, saying . . ." Ten quotations in Matthew appear
under this rubric, with minor variations,[8] and at least three other OT
quotations in the Gospel bear close affinities to this pattern of fulfillment
citation.[9] These authorial voiceovers highlight Matthew's strong interest
in the theme of fulfilled prophecy. Cumulatively, these passages appear
to frame Israel's Scripture—particularly the prophetic material—as a
predictive text pointing to events in the life of Jesus. And, on Matthew's
reading, the prophets are the mouthpieces of God. It is *God* who is the
divine Author plotting the script of history.

Matthew has front-loaded these formula quotations in the opening
chapters of his Gospel. Four of the ten formula quotations appear in the
birth and infancy narratives; if we add the fulfillment citations in 2:5-6
and 3:3, we find that nearly half of these weighty hermeneutical directives
are placed in the plot structure even before the baptism of Jesus, and still
another accompanies his initial proclamation of the kingdom in Galilee
(4:14-16). This cluster of fulfillment quotations near the beginning of the
Gospel conditions readers to expect that nearly everything in the story of
Jesus will turn out to be the fulfillment of something pre-scripted by God
through the prophets. Israel's sacred history is presented by Matthew as
an elaborate figurative tapestry designed to point forward to Jesus and his
activity.

And yet, precisely for that reason, we must reckon with a Matthean
hermeneutical program considerably more comprehensive than a collection of a dozen or so prooftexts. If Jesus has come to fulfill every jot and

tittle of the Law and the prophets (5:17-18), we should expect to discover a far more wide-ranging account of the accordance between Scripture and Gospel. And indeed, that is just what we find in Matthew's narrative: a diverse and complex use of Scripture. According to the tally complied by Donald Senior, there are *sixty-one* OT quotations in Matthew's Gospel.[10] That means that the formula quotations constitute, even by the most generous estimate, only about one-fifth of Matthew's total. And that does not even begin to reckon with the hundreds of more indirect OT allusions in the story.[11]

Above and beyond Matthew's citations of particular texts, we must reckon also with his repeated *figural readings of Scripture*, his deft narration of tales that Senior describes as "shadow stories from the Old Testament."[12] For example, the story of Herod's slaughter of the innocents contains no OT citations, but it surely echoes Pharaoh's decree to kill Hebrew children. And by so doing, it suggests that Herod, who claims the title "King of the Jews," is actually to be identified with Israel's ancient oppressor and that it is Jesus who is the true King of the Jews. Through this sort of figural narrative device, with or without explicit citation, Matthew leads the reader to *read backwards* and to see Jesus as the fulfillment of OT precursors, particularly Moses, David, and Isaiah's Servant figure.[13]

Jesus as Emmanuel: Matthew's Birth and Infancy Narrative

But over and above this Gospel's narration of Jesus as the typological fulfillment of the OT's kingly and prophetic figures, one distinctive feature of Matthew's narrative Christology is its bold identification of Jesus as Emmanuel, "God with us." This motif of Jesus as the manifestation of God's presence establishes the structural framework on which the story is built, as signaled by its appearance at the beginning, middle, and end of the story (1:23; 18:20; 28:20); these references frame and support everything in between. In contrast to Mark's circumspect indirection in identifying Jesus with the God of Israel, Matthew explicitly presents Jesus as the embodiment of divine presence in the world.[14]

"*God with us.*" This astounding claim about Jesus bursts onto the scene in the first of Matthew's fulfillment quotations. After a concise account of

Mary's unexpected pregnancy and Joseph's dream in which he is told by the angel of the Lord that her child is from the Holy Spirit, Matthew the narrator steps forward to explain:

> All this took place to fulfill what had been spoken by the Lord through the prophet:
>
>> "Look, the virgin shall conceive and bear a son,
>> and they shall name him Emmanuel,"
>> which means "God is with us." (Matt 1:22-23, citing Isa 7:14)

The history of interpretation has witnessed vigorous debate about Matthew's citation of Isaiah 7:14. Most of the controversy has centered upon the LXX's rendering of העלמה ("the young woman") as ἡ παρθένος ("the virgin"): Matthew follows the LXX, thereby facilitating his interpretation of Isaiah's prophecy as a prediction of a virgin birth.[15] Our present concern, however, is neither with the question of Mary's virginity nor with whether Matthew has illegitimately read the notion of a miraculous conception into Isaiah's prophecy. Rather, an intertextually attuned reading will focus attention on the way in which this Isaiah citation introduces Matthew's characterization of Jesus: he is not only the one who "will save his people from their sins" (1:21) but also—because his conception is "from the Holy Spirit" (1:18)—the one in whom God will be palpably present to his people (1:23).

Whatever we make of the complexities of Matthew's appropriation of Isaiah 7:14, his placement of this scriptural citation at the beginning of his narrative sounds a major keynote for his Gospel: Israel's God is now present to his people precisely in the person of Jesus. In order to consider what it means to say of Jesus that he is Emmanuel, and *in what sense* God is made manifest in him, we must continue on through the story. We find more clues just a little further on in Matthew's birth and infancy narrative.

"Out of Egypt . . ." In Matthew 2:13-15, Matthew offers a compressed account of the Holy Family's flight into Egypt and return after the death of Herod (2:13-15)—a tale unparalleled in the other Gospels. Matthew, reading backwards, sees in this episode a figural fulfillment of Israel's sojourn in bondage in Egypt and their subsequent return to the land of promise. Jesus becomes the one in whom the fate of Israel is embodied and enacted.[16] The key prophetic text adduced in the formula quotation

of 2:15 is drawn from Hosea 11:1: "When Israel was a child I loved him, and out of Egypt I called my son." This is a celebrated case in which Matthew does not follow the LXX, which reads, "out of Egypt have I called his children [τὰ τέκνα αὐτοῦ]." Matthew's predictive christological reading depends on a Greek text (τὸν υἱόν μου) that corresponds to the MT.[17] In context in Hosea, the "son" is clearly the people Israel as a whole; the sentence is not a prediction of a future messiah but a reference to past events of the exodus. Thus, Hosea's metaphor, referring to Israel corporately as God's "son," evokes a tradition that goes all the way back to God's instructing Moses to tell Pharaoh that "Israel is my firstborn son" (Exod 4:22-23). Matthew, however, transfigures Hosea's text by seeing it as a prefiguration of an event in the life of Jesus. Reading backwards, Matthew now sees the fate of God's "son" Israel recapitulated in the story of God's Son, Jesus: in both cases, the son is brought out of exile in Egypt back to the land.

If we examine the context of the Hosea citation in light of the framing Emmanuel motif, however, yet another layer of possible significance emerges. Hosea 11 is a text about God's compassion and faithfulness toward his chosen people, despite their waywardness. The climax of the passage is God's declared promise to be gracious:

> I will not execute my fierce anger;
> I will not again destroy Ephraim;
> for I am God and no mortal,
> *the Holy One in your midst,*
> and I will not come in wrath. (Hos 11:9)

This assurance of God's gracious presence "in your midst" is followed by a promise that God will bring his people back from exile:

> his children shall come trembling from the west.
> They shall come trembling like birds from Egypt,
> and like doves from the land of Assyria;
> and I will return them to their homes, says the LORD. (11:10b-11)

This example suggests that Matthew's formula quotations may have more narrative resonance and allusive subtlety than is often credited to them. Matthew cannot be unaware of the original contextual meaning of Hosea 11:1 as an expression of God's love for Israel—a love that persists even through Israel's subsequent unfaithfulness (Hos 11:8-9). Indeed,

Matthew's use of the quotation actually depends upon the reader's recognition of its original sense. Note carefully: if Hosea's words ("out of Egypt I called my son") were hermeneutically severed from reference to the original exodus story, the artful literary and theological effect of Matthew's narrative would be stifled. *The fulfillment of the prophet Hosea's words can be discerned only through an act of imagination that perceives the figural correspondence between the two stories of the exodus and the gospel.* Through the lens of Matthew's figural imagination, the two narrative patterns are projected on top of one another, so that the story of Jesus acquires the resonances of the story of Israel's deliverance.

The effect of the juxtaposition is to hint that Jesus now will carry the destiny of the people Israel, and that the outcome will be the rescue and vindication of Israel, as foreshadowed in the exodus story and brought to fulfillment in the resurrection of Jesus. The prophetic text from Hosea 11:1 functions as a middle term between the two stories, providing the hermeneutical clue that the exodus story is to be read as a figural template for God's action of choosing and saving his people, a template that can be applied to subsequent historical circumstances—whether God's mercy to disobedient Israel in Hosea's day or God's climactic rescue of his people Israel in the person of the Messiah Jesus.[18]

Thus, Hosea 11:1-11 resonates richly with the Matthean Emmanuel theme: the God who called his Son out of Egypt is the same God who is present *in their midst*. And Matthew has already disclosed that the form of God's presence is to be found in Jesus/Emmanuel. Matthew is beckoning his readers to interpret the homecoming of the Son out of Egypt as figuring forth the homecoming of Israel from exile (Hos 11:10-11), while *simultaneously* adumbrating the presence of Jesus as the presence of the God who calls them home and dwells in their midst (Hos 11:9).[19]

Rachel weeping and the new covenant. Once we are alerted to this figural dimension of Israel's story, we may then also hear additional resonances in the next brief unit of the birth narrative, the grim account of Herod's slaughter of the children of Bethlehem (2:16-18), which concludes with another formula quotation:

Then was fulfilled what had been spoken through the prophet Jeremiah:

A voice was heard in Ramah,
wailing and loud lamentation,

> Rachel weeping for her children;
> she refused to be consoled, because they are no more.
>
> (Matt 2:17-18)

Here it appears that the story of Israel, as Matthew carries it forward, is a story of suffering and lament. Ramah, in the book of Jeremiah, appears as a staging ground for the deportation of the Judean captives to Babylon (cf. Jer 40:1). Rachel, the wife of Jacob/Israel and therefore the figurative mother of the people as a whole,[20] mourns proleptically from the past over the exile—and, by implication, over the repeating pattern of violence against God's chosen. Herod's murder of the innocents takes its place alongside Pharaoh's decree against the Hebrew boy babies (Exod 1:15-22) and also alongside the defeat and exile of Judah in Jeremiah's time. Yet, recalling the latter story of exile, we may also hear an echo from the conclusion of Matthew's genealogy: "from the deportation to Babylon to the Messiah, fourteen generations" (1:17). Indeed, to recall Jeremiah's prophecy is necessarily to recall also its wider context:[21]

> Thus says the LORD:
> A voice is heard in Ramah,
> lamentation and bitter weeping.
> Rachel is weeping for her children;
> she refuses to be comforted for her children,
> because they are no more.
> Thus says the LORD:
> Keep your voice from weeping,
> and your eyes from tears;
> for there is a reward for your work,
> says the LORD:
> they shall come back from the land of the enemy;
> there is hope for your future,
> says the LORD:
> your children shall come back to their own country. (Jer 31:15-17)

If we are right to hear this echo of the wider context, this is a powerful example of the poetic device of *metalepsis*: the practice of citing a fragment that beckons readers to recover more of the original subtext in order to grasp the full force of the intertextual link. Jeremiah's image of Rachel weeping is a prelude to his bold prophecy of hope for the end of exile. Indeed, Jeremiah's oracle continues with an account of God's undying love for "Ephraim my dear son," promising that "I will surely have *mercy* on him" (Jer 31:18-20). That is the reason why there is hope for the future: violence and exile do not have the final word, for God's love for Israel will prevail and bring about restoration.

Surely it is not merely coincidental that in consecutive formula quotations (Matt 2:15 + 2:17-18) Matthew has linked these two very similar passages from Hosea 11:1-11 and Jeremiah 31:15-20. Both prophetic texts speak of the exile and suffering of an unfaithful people, and both declare that God will reach out in mercy and bring the people back from exile. By evoking just *these* prophecies in the infancy narrative, Matthew connects both the history and the future destiny of Israel to the figure of Jesus, and he hints that in Jesus—Emmanuel—the restoration of Israel is at hand. This suggests that Matthew is not merely looking for random Old Testament prooftexts that Jesus might somehow fulfill; rather, he is thinking about the *shape* of Israel's story and linking Jesus' life with key passages that promise God's unbreakable redemptive love for his people.[22]

That is why Matthew comments on Herod's slaughter of children by selecting a citation from the same chapter in Jeremiah that also promises "*a new covenant* with the house of Israel and the house of Judah" (Jer 31:31): Matthew's reference to Rachel works as a metaleptic trope, recalling the wider context of Jeremiah's prophecy.[23] Herod's murderous acts, then, function within Matthew's tale as a metaphor for all the history of Israel's grief and exile. Yet even in the dark moment of Rachel's grief, the echo of Jeremiah 31 offers comfort, beckoning God's people to lean forward into the hope of the days that are surely coming when God—in the person of Jesus—will have *mercy*, bring back the exiles, and write the Law on their hearts.

Jesus as the Divine Presence

Worshiping Jesus. Because Matthew closely follows Mark's narrative outline of Jesus' Galilean ministry, many of the same stories that in Mark imply Jesus' identity with God function similarly in Matthew. For example, Matthew retells the story of Jesus stilling the storm (8:23-27) in a way that closely parallels Mark 4:35-41. If anything, Matthew more strongly hints at Jesus' divine status in the words the disciples use to address him when they wake him up in the midst of the storm.

Mark 4:38: "Teacher, do you not care that we are perishing?"
Matthew 8:25: "Lord, save us [κύριε, σῶσον]! We are perishing!"

The exclamation in Matthew takes on the form of an urgent prayer to Jesus as the Lord, a prayer for deliverance. In the thematically related story of Jesus walking on the sea (Mark 6:45-52 / Matt 14:22-33), Matthew not only expands the tale to include an account of Peter's attempt to join Jesus in walking on the waves but, most tellingly, writes a different ending to the story. When Jesus finally gets into the boat, the astonished Markan disciples, the reader is told, fail to understand because their hearts are hardened (Mark 6:51-52); the Matthean disciples, on the other hand, *worship* him, saying, " 'Truly you are the Son of God' " (Matt 14:33). It is difficult to imagine a clearer illustration of Matthew's didactic remolding of the tradition. Whereas Mark's enigmatic story summons readers to awe-filled meditation on the mystery of Jesus' identity, Matthew reimagines the water-crossing as a clear parable of Jesus' relation to the church: the worship of the disciples anticipates and represents the worship eventually to be given to the Risen Lord, to whom all authority in heaven and on earth has been given. But both stories—the storm-stilling and the water-walking—rest on a common OT substratum: there is only One who can command the wind and storm, only One who can stride across the waves. Matthew receives the scriptural message encoded in the Markan mystery and brings it to more explicit expression for the instruction of his readers. The worship of the disciples acknowledges and declares Jesus' identity with the one God of Israel, present in the midst of his people.

The action of the disciples in worshiping Jesus (προσκύνησαν αὐτῷ) is only one of numerous incidents in this Gospel where various characters are depicted in the posture of worshiping him: the magi (2:2, 11), a leper seeking healing (8:2), a ruler of the synagogue (9:18), the Canaanite woman (15:25), the mother of James and John (20:20), the two Marys who first encounter the Risen Lord (28:9), and the disciples at the resurrection appearance on a mountain in Galilee (28:17). Now, to be sure, the verb προσκυνεῖν possesses a certain ambiguity. It can in some contexts mean "pay homage, bow down," without necessarily implying a divine status of the one who receives the gesture of homage. Several of these Matthean passages might be understood in such a sense, particularly in the cases of those who come to Jesus as postulants.[24] Yet in view of Matthew's portrayal of Jesus as "God with us" and his use of the verb in settings where it unmistakably narrates an appropriate human response to Jesus' epiphanic self-manifestation (14:33; 28:9; 28:17), it would appear that in and through these references to worshiping Jesus, Matthew is identifying him as nothing less than the embodied presence of Israel's God, the one to whom alone worship is due, the one who jealously forbids the worship of any idols, images, or other gods.

Indeed, the clinching argument for this reading is to be found in the story of the devil's temptation of Jesus in the wilderness. The devil offers Jesus all the kingdoms of the world if Jesus will only fall down and worship him (προσκυνήσεις), but Jesus repels this seduction by a ringing quotation of Deuteronomy 6:13 LXX: "The Lord your God you shall worship [προσκυνήσεις] and him alone you shall serve" (Matt 4:9-10). Once this commandment has been forcefully set forth in the narrative, readers have little choice but to interpret Jesus' acceptance of worship (προσκυνήσις) from other characters as an implicit acknowledgment of his divine identity.

A similar point is made in Matthew's supplementation of the Markan controversy story about plucking grain on the sabbath (Mark 2:23-28 / Matt 12:1-8). To the argument about a Davidic precedent, Matthew's Jesus adds a halakhic argument about priests who work on the sabbath in the Temple and yet are blameless (referring to the prescribed sabbath offerings, Num 28:9-10). But the punch line—the assertion that makes sense of this argument—is that "something greater than the Temple is here" (Matt 12:6). We are not told precisely what the "something greater" might be, but the inference lies readily at hand that it must be Jesus himself.[25] What could be greater than the Temple other than the one to whom it is dedicated, the one who is worshiped in it? Matthew's argument is in effect this: if Jesus is "God with us," then his presence sanctifies the labors of those who work to serve him, even on the sabbath. Indeed, if Jesus is "God with us," then his personal presence now takes the place of the Temple where the presence of God was formerly thought to dwell.[26] Writing his Gospel in the aftermath of the catastrophic destruction of the Temple in Jerusalem, Matthew affirms that Jesus' presence is "greater than the Temple" and thereby offers powerful reassurance for his followers as well as a provocative challenge to those who reject him.

Where two or three are together. The Emmanuel theme surfaces dramatically again in the fourth of the five great teaching discourses in

Matthew's Gospel, Jesus' teaching on church discipline and forgiveness (18:1-35). After giving instruction about how the ἐκκλησία is to deal with offenders (18:15-17), Jesus promises to the community the authority to bind and loose both on earth and in heaven (18:18-19). The warrant for this extraordinary promise is given by Jesus in his pledge of continuing presence with the gathered community: "For where two or three are gathered in my name, I am there among them" (18:20). Commentators have long noted the close parallel between this word of Jesus and a reassuring promise about Torah study articulated by the rabbis in the Mishnah: "If two or three sit together and words of the Torah [are spoken] between them, the Divine Presence [Shekinah] rests between them" (m.'Aboth 3:2).

It is difficult to know whether one of these two claims is dependent upon or reactive against the other. If Matthew has modeled this Jesus saying (Matt 18:20) on an older rabbinic tradition about the Torah, then for his Gospel Jesus takes the place of the Law, and his continuing presence in the community occupies the place previously accorded to the Shekinah—the rabbinic designation for the glorious presence of God that accompanied Israel in the wilderness, as manifested in the tabernacle. If, on the other hand, the Mishnah's saying postdates Matthew's Gospel, then perhaps the rabbis were seeking to counteract what they regarded as a blasphemous claim of the early Christians that Jesus could somehow embody God's presence, by asserting an alternative claim about the Torah as the effective agent mediating divine presence to the people of God.[27] In either case, both sayings, Matthean and Mishnaic, represent hermeneutical adaptations in the irrevocably changed situation after 70 C.E. Once the Temple has been destroyed and the holy of holies no longer stands in a building made with hands, the community must seek to discern how the God of all the earth will be made known in the world. In this situation, Matthew emphatically locates the divine presence in the figure of Jesus himself, who promises (in a saying that anticipates the resurrection and the ending of the Gospel) to be forever present wherever his followers gather and invoke his name. In short, in Matthew 18:20 Jesus now declares himself, for the first time, to be the Emmanuel promised in the narrator's opening fulfillment citation in 1:23.

"My words will not pass away." Precisely because Jesus is Emmanuel, in his subsequent discourse on the end of the age (Matthew 24) he can offer the further remarkable assurance that his words will outlast all creation: "Heaven and earth will pass away, but my words will not pass away" (24:35). If we ask ourselves who might legitimately say such a thing, once again there can be only one answer: we find ourselves face-to-face with the God of the Old Testament. Isaiah gives definitive expression to this theological truth:

> The grass withers, the flower fades,
> when the breath of the LORD blows upon it;
> surely the people are grass.
> The grass withers, the flower fades;
> but *the word of our God will stand forever.* (Isa 40:7-8)

Christian interpreters lulled by familiarity with Matthew's Gospel may not fully appreciate the immense scope of the christological assertions made at every turn by Matthew. But there can be no doubt that the word spoken by Jesus in Matthew 24:35 can be true only if it really is "the word of our God," only if the speaker who says "my words will not pass away" is in fact the God of Israel, God with us.

Jesus' presence in the poor. And yet—alongside these mind-boggling claims that portray Jesus as greater than the Temple, worthy of the worship that belongs to God alone, able to speak a word that transcends time and space—Matthew also proclaims Jesus' presence among his people in the form of the poor and the suffering. In the climactic unit that concludes the teachings of Jesus in this Gospel, Matthew creates an *inclusio* with the Beatitudes of 5:3-12 by narrating an unsettling last judgment scene in which Jesus/Emmanuel turns out to have been present among us in the hungry and thirsty and naked and sick and imprisoned of this world (25:31-46). This, too, is an integral part of what "God with us" means in Matthew, as exemplified in the story of Jesus' own suffering, culminating in the cross. To recognize God's presence truly, then, Matthew's readers must serve the needs of the poor, for "just as you did it to one of the least of these my brothers, you did it to me" (25:40).[28]

Where could such an idea originate, the notion that caring for the poor (or, alternatively, Jesus' poor followers) is somehow equivalent to encountering the presence of God? Just at this point, Israel's wisdom tradition casts an unexpected shaft of illumination upon the identity of Jesus: "Whoever is kind to the poor lends to the LORD, and will be repaid in full" (Prov 19:17). Matthew does not quote this text, and there is no obvious verbal echo of it in Matthew 25, though the LXX rendering of Proverbs 19:17 employs language characteristic of Matthew's concerns and emphases: ὁ ἐλεῶν πτωχόν ("the one who *has mercy* on the poor man"). Nonetheless, Matthew's account of the final judgment stands in continuity with this fundamental insight of Israel's sages, as articulated in the Proverbs text: we will be judged and recompensed in accordance with our treatment of the poor.[29] But the most remarkable link here between Proverbs and Matthew lies in the former's affirmation that those who show mercy to the poor are in effect lending *to the Lord*. This is precisely what Matthew reaffirms and elaborates: it is the Lord Jesus who is the ultimate recipient of human acts of kindness. If the connection between Proverbs 19:17 and Matthew 25:40 be granted, a crucial corollary follows: when Jesus says that mercy shown to the poor is really shown to him, he is placing himself directly into the role of the Lord referred to by Proverbs— that is, the Lord God of Israel. In the context of Matthew 25, this makes perfect sense, for the mysterious lowly figure to whom mercy was (or was not) shown is also portrayed as eschatological judge of the nations, the Son of Man (25:31-33) whose destiny is to sit at the right hand of Power, coming on the clouds of heaven as prophesied in Daniel 7:13-14 (cf. Matt 26:64). Thus, an intertextual reading of Matthew's last judgment scene alongside Proverbs 19:17 has the unexpected effect of underlining once again the identity of Jesus with the God of Israel.[30]

The Promise of Jesus' Presence to the End of the Age

All of Matthew's prior pointers to Jesus' identity with God come to their *telos* in the words of reassurance with which his Gospel ends: "And behold, I am with you all the days until the end of the age" (28:20). No merely human figure could offer such an extravagant promise of eternal presence; the very content of this comforting word implies the divine identity of the one who speaks it. But, beyond the simple logical implications of Jesus' parting promise, its significance is amplified by the extensive network of scriptural intertexts that it evokes. David Kupp enumerates in the MT and LXX "at least 114 instances" of a formula "promising or asserting that God is 'with' an individual, a group, or the nation Israel."[31] It is not possible to study all these examples here, but we may focus in particular on three passages whose verbal formulation most closely resembles the concluding words of Matthew, asking in each case what the resultant intertextual echo might contribute to our appreciation of Matthew's account of Jesus' identity.

First, hearers of Matthew's ending might well perceive reverberations of the promise spoken by God in Jacob's dream at Bethel in Genesis 28:12-17 (emphasis added, and key parallels between Matthew and the LXX text noted where appropriate):

> And he dreamed that there was a ladder set up on the earth, the top of it reaching to heaven; and the angels of God were ascending and descending on it. *And the* LORD *stood beside him* [cf. Matt 28:18a] and said, "I am the LORD, the God of Abraham your father and the God of Isaac; the land on which you lie I will give to you and to your offspring; and your offspring shall be like the dust of the earth, and you shall spread abroad to the west and to the east and to the north and to the south; and all the families of the earth [πᾶσαι αἱ φυλαὶ τῆς γῆς; cf. Matt 28:19: πάντα τὰ ἔθνη] shall be blessed in you and in your offspring. ***Know that I am with you*** [ἰδοὺ ἐγὼ μετὰ σοῦ] and will keep you wherever you go [ἐν τῇ ὁδῷ πάσῃ], and will bring you back to this land; for *I will not leave you* until I have done what I have promised you." Then Jacob woke from his sleep and said, "Surely the LORD is in this place—and I did not know it!" And he was afraid [ἐφοβήθη], and said, "How awesome is this place! This is none other than the house of God, and this is the gate of heaven."

The clearest link between this promissory passage and Jesus' final words in Matthew is found in their similar formulas announcing divine presence:

Genesis 28:15: καὶ ἰδοὺ ἐγὼ μετὰ σοῦ
Matthew 28:20: καὶ ἰδοὺ ἐγὼ μεθ' ὑμῶν εἰμι

(The change from the singular σοῦ to the plural ὑμῶν is, of course, dictated by the different narrative settings, though in different ways both Jacob and the eleven disciples are to be understood as representing Israel corporately.) But apart from the direct verbal parallel, there are other noteworthy similarities. In both texts, the Lord comes and stands in the presence of the hearers. Jacob is told that "all the tribes of the earth" will find blessing through him, while the Eleven are told to go with good news to "all the nations/Gentiles." In both texts, the recipients of revelation greet it with fear and worship. The promise that the Lord will bring Jacob "back to this land" is closely bound together with the theme of the end of exile, which we have encountered throughout Matthew's story from the beginning. But most significantly, in both texts, the Lord speaks in the first person and promises continuing presence:

> Genesis 28: "Behold I am with you. . . . I will not leave you until I have done what I have promised you."
> Matthew 28: "Behold I am with you all the days until the end of the age."

The parallel cries out for readers to draw an obvious christological conclusion: in the ending of Matthew, Jesus now stands in the same role occupied by the Lord God in Jacob's dream.

A different emphasis emerges in our second example. At the beginning of the book of Jeremiah, we find a call/commissioning narrative, in which the youthful Jeremiah is appointed by God as "a prophet to the nations" (Jer 1:5; LXX: προφήτην εἰς ἔθνη). He protests that he is only a boy and does not know what to say. And this is the response he receives from the Lord:

> "Do not say, 'I am only a boy':
> for you shall go to all to whom I send you,
> and you shall speak whatever I command [πάντα ὅσα ἐὰν ἐντείλωμαί] you.
> Do not be afraid of them,
> for I am with you [μετὰ σοῦ ἐγώ εἰμι] to deliver you, says the Lord."
>
> (Jer 1:7-8)

Whereas God's speech in Jacob's dream was chiefly a word of promise, this passage resembles the ending of Matthew in focusing on the *mission* of the one who receives the word of revelation. Like Jeremiah, the disciples in Matthew 28 (even those who hesitate, v. 17) are commissioned and sent *to the nations*. Like Jeremiah who is ordered to speak "whatever I command you," the disciples are to teach the nations to keep "all things whatever I have commanded you" (πάντα ὅσα ἐνετειλάμην ὑμῖν). And in both texts, the ground for confidence in this ambitious mission is simply the promise "I am with you." Once again, Matthew's story seems to give Jesus the same line to speak that in the Old Testament belongs to God.

The final intertext to consider is found in the book of the prophet Haggai. The prophecies of this book are set in the period immediately following the end of the Babylonian exile. The returned exiles, though unsure of themselves, have tentatively begun the work of rebuilding the ruined Temple. It is in this context that the word of the Lord comes to the people:

Then Haggai, the messenger of the LORD, spoke to the people with the
LORD's message, saying, I am with you [ἐγώ εἰμι μεθ' ὑμῶν], says the LORD.
(Hag 1:13)

A month later, Haggai goes on to repeat this same word of reassurance,
encouraging the people to continue working on the building, "for I am
with you, says the LORD of hosts" (2:4). This time the presence formula
is supplemented by a reminder of the promise given to Israel "when you
came up out of Egypt" and an additional promise: "My spirit abides among
you; do not fear" (2:5). Here, the most interesting parallels have to do with
Haggai's postexilic setting, corresponding analogically to the immediate
postresurrection setting of Matthew's ending. Haggai's repeated assurance
of God's presence in this moment of fragile hope serves to strengthen the
resolve of the people for the work to which they are called—just as Jesus'
final assurance provides a warrant for the disciples to proceed confidently
to the mission on which Jesus is sending them. Indeed, Haggai's word of
encouragement might have had special resonance for a late first-century
community of Jesus' followers, living in the immediate aftermath of the
destruction of the Temple in Jerusalem. In this case, however, they are
called not to rebuild an edifice to house the presence of God but rather to
recognize the living presence of God in the one who stands before them
and promises, just as God had promised five hundred years before, to be
present and to sustain their labors. As in the other examples just reviewed,
we see that once again it is *Jesus* who now utters the reassuring promise
of divine presence, thereby embodying the divine role in his own person.

Pushing the Boundaries

Despite the evidence we have outlined, many readers might hestitate to
draw the conclusions I have been suggesting. After all, Matthew's Jesus,
like Mark's, professes ignorance about the day and hour of the apocalyptic endtime events (24:36). He prays urgently to be spared from drinking
the cup of suffering and death but finally submits his will to the will of
his Father (26:36-46).[32] And in his death agony on the cross, he screams
out the same cry of dereliction that Mark had narrated: "My God, my
God, why have you forsaken me?" (27:46). Surely these details of the narrative would seem to contradict any claim of Jesus' sharing in the divine
identity?

It is noteworthy, however, that each of these elements that would seem to posit a distinction between Jesus and God is incorporated by Matthew from Mark's narrative. He has *preserved* these narrative details from his source while at the same time *adding* much material to make Mark's affirmation of Jesus' divine identity more explicit and robust.[33] In short, Matthew's redactional tendency is to strengthen the claim of Jesus' divine identity, without erasing the Markan narrative elements that would complicate such a claim. The Markan "non-identity" material is embedded within Matthew's overtly heightened Christology. And, like Mark, Matthew gives no explanation for the resulting tension. This finding is consistent with a general Matthean tolerance for dialectical tensions (e.g., the tension between stern moral demand and infinite grace for those who fall short of obedience).[34] Matthew's narrative style is synthetic but not systematic: he works differing traditions into his story without seeking to resolve them at a conceptual level.

These findings underscore Rowan Williams' observation that the "reorganization of religious language" after the cross and resurrection was "a centuries-long task." Matthew played a key role in shaping the trajectory of that task, but he did not have—despite the triadic baptismal formula in 28:19—a fully worked-out Trinitarian theology. His narrative portrayal of Jesus is one of the most important sources and inspirations for the ultimate outworking of the Chalcedonian christological doctrine, but he does not himself articulate such a doctrine in propositional terms.

It remains clear, nonetheless, that Matthew the Evangelist proclaims and shows again and again that Jesus is the embodiment of Israel's God in human form. Even before his birth, Jesus is identified by Matthew as Emmanuel, God with us. And after his resurrection he speaks in fulfillment of precisely that identity: he possesses all authority in heaven and on earth, and he promises his sustaining presence throughout all time in all places, as he sends his followers out to summon all nations to obey him. There is only One who can speak such things truthfully.

At just this point, David Kupp, whose wide-ranging and astute readings have done much to illuminate the central importance of the Emmanuel motif in Matthean Christology, begins to back away from the radical implications of his own analysis. He writes:

Nowhere in Matthew's portrayal are Jesus and God simply identified. Jesus' self-perception throughout the Gospel is clearly within the hier-archical relationship of the Son to his Father (even within the triadic baptismal formula in 28:19). . . . For Matthew, Yʜᴡʜ is the only true God, and worship of Jesus his Son, the Emmanuel Messiah, is a christo-logical window to his divine agency of his Father's will. Worship of Jesus in Matthew does not conflict with worship of God, but is his followers' way of recognizing Jesus' divine sonship and God's presence among them in Jesus, i.e., some kind of perceptual equivalence between them.[35]

Kupp is correct to say that Jesus and God are not *simply* identified; the identification is complex and worked out through the medium of narra-tive, particularly through the overlapping intertextual patterns we have traced, some overt and some subtle. By the same token, however, it is far too simple to say that the relation between the Father and the Son is hier-archical or subordinationist; Matthew's narrative offers, as we have seen, far too many clues of a richer unity in identity. And to speak of a "chris-tological window" that relates Jesus to Yʜᴡʜ merely in terms of "agency" or "perceptual equivalence" is at once to superimpose foreign categories upon Matthew's text and to subvert the explosive theological logic of the story. Indeed, if we may press the point, it is to suggest that the disciples who worship Jesus in 14:33, 28:9, and 28:17 are actually guilty not only of a category mistake but of idolatry.

Matthew highlights the worship of Jesus for one reason: he believes and proclaims that Jesus *is* the embodied presence of God and that to worship him *is* to worship Yʜᴡʜ—not merely an agent or a facsimile or an intermediary. If we read the story within the hermeneutical matrix of Israel's Scripture, we can draw no other conclusion. Thus, Matthew's "reorganization of Israel's religious language" comes to its most intense focus at this point. Not only does Matthew proclaim, as Rowan Williams notes, that the crucifixion of Jesus was "the event that somehow brought God's salvation to the world." Matthew has a more radical claim to offer: the one who was crucified and raised from the dead is himself the embod-iment of the God who rules over all creation and abides with his people forever.

4

The One Who Redeems Israel
Reading Scripture with Luke

"We had hoped that he was the one . . ."

In the final chapter of Luke's Gospel, we meet two new characters, Cleopas and an unnamed companion, despondently trudging away from Jerusalem toward the village of Emmaus (Luke 24:13-35).[1] The crucifixion of their leader, Jesus, has dashed their hopes. They had dared to hope that he might be the urgently awaited messianic figure who would rescue Israel from oppression, but his swift and brutal execution by the Roman imperial forces had doomed that expectation—or so they thought. In a scene of exquisite dramatic irony, the risen Jesus appears and walks with them, unrecognized. He asks what they are discussing, and Cleopas, comically oblivious to the identity of this new traveling companion, replies, "Are you the only stranger visiting Jerusalem who doesn't know what has been happening in these days?"

The ironic gap between Cleopas' presumption of superior knowledge and his actual ignorance of Jesus' identity prepares the reader (who has been clearly informed by the narrator in verses 15-16 that the stranger is Jesus) to interpret the dialogue that follows as a hermeneutical corrective to the preresurrectional understanding of Jesus that the Emmaus pilgrims articulate.

They describe him as "a man, a prophet powerful in deed and word before God and all the people" (24:19). Despite his prophetic powers, however, Jesus had been put to death by the chief priests and rulers—hence, the disappointment of these disciples' fervent expectation: "But we had hoped that he was the one to redeem [λυτροῦσθαι] Israel" (24:21).

These poignant words recall precisely the expectation aroused in the glad songs of the Gospel's birth narrative. Zechariah, filled with the Holy Spirit, had declared it in these terms:

> Blessed be the Lord, the God of Israel,
> for he has visited his people and made redemption [λύτρωσιν] for them.
> And he has raised up a horn of salvation for us
> in the house of his servant David. (Luke 1:68-69)

Consequently, the wistful lament of the Emmaus disciples retraces the experience of the sympathetic first-time reader who has followed the story closely. Why has Israel seemingly not been redeemed? Why, such a reader might ask, have we not yet found "salvation from our enemies and from the hand of all who hate us" (1:71)? The death of Jesus appears to confirm that those enemies still have Israel's fate firmly in their grip. Even the report that some women had found the tomb empty has seemed to Cleopas and friend nothing more than a puzzling oddity, the account perhaps of a religious "vision" but nothing like the new messianic kingdom for which they had been hoping (24:22-24).

Much hangs, then, on Jesus' reply:

> And he said to them, "O foolish and slow of heart to trust in all that the prophets spoke! Weren't these things necessary: for the Messiah to suffer and enter into his glory?" And beginning from Moses and from all the prophets, he thoroughly interpreted for them *the things concerning himself in all the Scriptures.* (24:25-27)

Luke's sketchy summary is tantalizing, for it does not explain exactly how "all the Scriptures" might be read as testimony to Jesus. The effect of this episode is to bring us up short and send us back to the beginning of the Gospel to *reread* it, in hopes of discerning more clearly how the identity and mission of Jesus might be prefigured in Israel's Scripture. And such a rereading will of course require a rereading of Israel's Scripture as well. This second reading of the Gospel and Scripture together will be a retrospective reading in light of the resurrection.[2] We will be *reading backwards*, seeking to find previously hidden figural correspondences between "Moses and the prophets" and the mysterious stranger who chastises us as "slow of heart" for failing to discover such correspondences on our first reading.

The dramatic irony of Luke's Emmaus story implies that if we understand the scriptural witness about the Messiah, we will perceive that he is more than "a prophet powerful in deed and word before God and all the people." That is the true but limited preliminary understanding of Cleopas and his friend,[3] an understanding that the veiled risen Jesus now seeks to correct.

Yet—and here we encounter another layer of irony—it has become the conventional view of modern NT criticism that the Gospel of Luke represents a "low" or "primitive" Christology. According to this view, Luke portrays Jesus as a Spirit-anointed prophet, a teacher of divine wisdom, and a righteous martyr. Lacking, however, are any doctrines of preexistence and incarnation; lacking is any clear assertion of Jesus' identity with God.[4] In short, most NT critics have ascribed to Luke a Christology remarkably similar to that of the Emmaus travelers! Sometimes it is suggested that Luke carefully respects his historical sources by keeping references to any superhuman status of Jesus out of his Gospel and reserving all "high" christological affirmations for the Acts of the Apostles, after the resurrection.[5] As the Emmaus story suggests, however, an attentive reading of Luke's Gospel gives us substantial reason to question this characterization of Lukan Christology.

Luke's Intertextual Narrative Technique:
An Overview

Any assessment of Luke's understanding of the identity of Jesus must reckon with the *narrative* mode of the presentation. It will hardly do to extract a list of titles for Jesus that Luke employs in the Gospel and then extrapolate propositional statements about Luke's Christology.[6] Rather, we come to know Jesus in Luke only as his *narrative identity* is enacted in and through the story.[7] An important element of Luke's narrative art lies in the way in which he evokes echoes of Israel's Scripture and thereby leads readers to a complex, intertextually formed perception of his central character. This is the decisive heremeneutical clue given in the final chapter of Luke's Gospel, as Jesus "opens the Scriptures" to his followers. They had hoped he was "the one to redeem Israel." If, as Luke's ironic tale implies, they were wrong to judge that hope disappointed, then the key to understanding *how* Jesus redeems Israel must be found in a renewed scripturally shaped understanding of Jesus as Israel's redeemer.

I would like to propose that a careful reading of Luke's narrative, with particular attention to its intertextual relation with the OT, discloses that—no less than Mark and Matthew—he subtly but insistently portrays Jesus as the embodied presence of Israel's Lord and God. This interpretation of Jesus' *divine identity*[8] in Luke has been suggested by a few scholars—most compellingly by C. Kavin Rowe[9]—but it stands sharply in contrast to most modern critical readings of Lukan Christology. It will therefore be necessary to consider the evidence for this reading of Luke at greater length.

Luke's narrative design unfolds the pattern of promise and fulfillment with graceful skill. Scriptural intertexts appear chiefly in two ways. First, in Luke's Gospel direct citations of Scripture are almost always found *in the mouths of characters* in the story, not in overt authorial commentary.[10] This narrative device imparts to Luke's intertextual citations a *dramatic* character; readers are required to interpret the intertextual relations in light of the narrative's unfolding plot. To take a leading example, to which we shall return later in our discussion, the meaning of Isaiah 61:1-2 in Luke's account is shaped by Luke's placement of the words in the mouth of Jesus at the inauguration of his activity in Galilee, as he begins his ministry of healing and teaching with a public proclamation in the synagogue in Nazareth (Luke 4:16-21). The number of these explicit quotations, however, is surprisingly small, though many more are to be found in the second volume of the story, the Acts of the Apostles.

But, in Luke's Gospel itself, most of the intertextual references are, instead, of a second kind: *implicit correspondences, suggested* through the literary devices of allusion and echo. To be sure, the opening two chapters of the Gospel create a vivid expectation of the fulfillment of scriptural promise, and the concluding resurrection appearance stories assert forthrightly that Moses and the prophets and the Psalms are somehow fulfilled in Jesus (24:25-27, 44-47). Yet, in between these signposts, the narrative offers, for the most part, only elusive hints and reminiscences of OT precursors.[11] The effect of this narrative technique is to lure us into the work of close, retrospectively alert reading, seeking to read backwards, to discern and interpret the intertextual clues woven into the fabric of the story.

Luke's diction and imagery repeatedly evoke fragmentary Old Testament prefigurations of the story of Jesus. We might picture his narrative technique in the following way: it is as though the primary action of the

Gospel is played out on center stage, in front of the footlights, while a screen at the back of the stage displays a kaleidoscopic series of flickering sepia-toned images from Israel's Scripture. The images can flash by almost unnoticed; however, if the viewer pays careful attention, there are many moments in which the words or gestures of the characters onstage mirror something in the shifting backdrop (or is it the other way around?). At such moments of synchronicity, the viewer may experience a flash of hermeneutical insight, as the "live action" recapitulates a scene from the older story, allowing the two narrative moments to interpret one another. But it is not Luke's style to develop sustained sequences in which the patterns coincide and run parallel; rather, almost as soon as we recognize one such narrative convergence, the moment has passed, and a different image appears on the backdrop, perhaps suggesting an entirely different set of linkages. For purposes of analysis, we can freeze the action and study it slowly. But that is not the effect created for the reader or hearer of Luke's narrative. The story keeps moving and leaves us with a powerful but indistinct sense of analogy between God's saving acts for Israel in the past and the new liberating events coming to fulfillment in the story of Jesus.[12]

Thus, many of the OT echoes in Luke do not function as direct typological prefigurations of events in the life of Jesus. Still less do they function as prooftexts. Rather, they create a broader and subtler effect: they create a narrative world thick with scriptural memory. The Gospel scenes are played out on a stage with scenery familiar to the reader who remembers the biblical drama. The things that happen in Luke are the *kinds* of things that happened in the tales of the patriarchs and prophets, and the plotted action, while never simply identical to the OT stories, is often suggestively reminiscent of Israel's sacred past. It is as though we are hearing, throughout Luke's Gospel, subtle musical variations on a theme. Most significantly, the memories evoked by retrospective reading disclose that the character of God portrayed in this Gospel is consistent with his character as displayed throughout Israel's history: this God who elects Israel, judges their faithlessness, and still acts in unexpected ways to redeem them is recognizably the same God the reader knows from previous episodes of the story—but now made manifest in new and surprising ways. The question before us, then, is *how* Israel's God is manifest in and through the figure of Jesus.

Intimations of Divine Identity Christology
in Luke's Gospel

Jesus as the Son of God. Luke makes it clear from the opening scenes of his narrative that his central character, Jesus, has a divine origin and that he is no ordinary human figure; the angel Gabriel announces to Mary that her child is to be "the Son of the Most High" (1:32). The careful reader will note the contrast to John, who will be called "*the prophet* of the Most High" (1:76). "Son of the Most High" is not merely an honorific royal title, for Luke carefully informs us that Jesus is to be born to a virgin mother (1:27, 34) and that his conception will occur through the agency of the Holy Spirit, who will "overshadow" Mary. The angel Gabriel's pronouncement then spells out the implications of this miraculous birth: "Therefore the child to be born will also be called holy, God's Son" (1:35).[13] After the trumpet-flourish of this portentous introduction, it is hard to see how any reader could suppose that Luke has a "low" Christology or that the Jesus who will subsequently appear in the story could be rightly interpreted as only an inspired prophet. (At this point, it would seem that the interpretative instincts of untutored Christian readers have usually been better than those of learned Lukan scholars who have bracketed this scene out as somehow less than definitive for understanding Luke's Christology.) Jesus enters history through supernatural means, and he is therefore God's Son in some mysterious but real fashion; his sonship is not a matter of honorific attribution or adoption.

The identification of Jesus as Son of God is reinforced in Luke's accounts of the baptism of Jesus and the transfiguration. At both of these pivotal dramatic events, a voice from heaven speaks, identifying Jesus as "my Son, the beloved" (3:22) and "my Son, the chosen one" (9:35).[14] Each of these passages in turn evokes a chorus of scriptural echoes. In the case of "my Son, the beloved," the dominant voice in the chorus is the allusion to Isaac in Genesis 22, though when the heavenly voice continues the acclamation by saying, "in you I am well pleased," there is an additional echo of God's address to the Servant in Isaiah 42:1: "Here is my servant, whom I uphold, my chosen, in whom my soul delights." This second echo is amplified into a more explicit allusion in the transfiguration passage with its reference to the Son as the "chosen one" (ὁ ἐκλελεγμένος). In the LXX, Isaiah 42:1 is explicitly interpreted as a prophecy concerning Jacob, understood as a corporate designation for "Israel, my chosen one" (ὁ ἐκλεκτός μου). And, in both of these passages, the royal messianic Psalm 2:7 may reverberate more distantly in the background. While the OT allusions in the baptism and transfiguration texts would seem to identify Jesus with Israel, God's covenant partner rather than God himself, we must recall that Luke regularly weaves together different strands of material and that no one image identifying Jesus should be understood as exclusive of others. Indeed, when these texts are read in narrative sequence with Luke 1:26-38, the effect is to suggest that Jesus' status as Son entails some sort of identity both with God and with Israel/humanity.[15]

The theme of Jesus' sonship surfaces again in the striking prayer of 10:21-22, the so-called *Jubelruf* ("joyful shout"), in which Jesus suddenly blurts out an expression of intimacy with God the Father that would be immediately at home in John's Gospel:[16]

> At that same hour Jesus rejoiced in the Holy Spirit and said, "I thank you, Father, Lord of heaven and earth, because you have hidden these things from the wise and the intelligent and have revealed them to infants; yes, Father, for such was your gracious will. All things have been handed over to me by my Father; and no one knows who the Son is except the Father, or who the Father is except the Son and anyone to whom the Son chooses to reveal him."

At first glance this effusion appears incongruous with Jesus' manner of speaking in the bulk of the synoptic traditions (though this is in fact one of the double-tradition passages that Luke shares with Matthew [Matt 11:25-27]). But on closer reflection, this expression of privileged filial relation to God is entirely consonant with other material in Luke. In addition to the Son of God references in the annunciation, the baptism, and the transfiguration accounts, we might recall the boyhood story in which Jesus replies to the scolding of his anxious parents by shrugging and saying, "Didn't you know that I must be in my Father's house?" (2:49). Likewise, in the wilderness temptation story, Jesus' successful rebuff of the devil shows that he is truly the Son of God, in a way that rejects the false demonstrations proposed by the tempter (4:1-13).[17]

Jesus' affirmation in Luke 10:22 that "all things have been handed over to me by my Father" serves well as an explanation of his astonishing power to heal and his right to confer on his disciples authority over demons—as confirmed by the immediately preceding narrative unit

(10:17-20). This same power to confer divine authority is reiterated at the scene of Jesus' final supper with the disciples, when he says to them: "You are the ones who have remained with me throughout my testings. And I confer upon you, just as my Father has conferred upon me, a kingdom, so that you might eat and drink at my table in my kingdom. And you will sit on thrones, judging the twelve tribes of Israel" (22:28-30). Elsewhere in the story, Jesus has spoken of "the kingdom of God," but now it becomes "*my* kingdom." It is also pertinent to note that Jesus is not himself one of the twelve tribal heads of the new Israel that he envisions; rather, he is the one who appoints the Twelve as judges, and so he stands in a position of superior authority.[18] Lastly, even *in extremis* Jesus continues to pray to his Father and to commit his life into God's hands (23:46).

All of this evidence is consistent with the portrayal of the Father/Son relation in the prayer of Luke 10:21-22: it is a relation of special mutual knowledge that results in Jesus' reception of authority over all things, including the power to reveal the identity of the Father and to confer divine authority upon others. Thus, this interlude in the narrative functions as a dramatic soliloquy, in which Jesus steps from behind a momentarily closed curtain and prays in a way that is meant to be overheard by the audience. This overheard prayer provides crucial clues that help the audience, in turn, to make sense of the rest of the action on stage both before and after the soliloquy. It is in light of Jesus' special identity as Son of God that the otherwise astounding claims and events of the drama become comprehensible.

Thus, no matter what studies of tradition history might show about the history of religious background of "Son of God" as a royal title,[19] the significance of this language *within Luke's narrative* cannot be simply restricted to the realm of royal messianic expectation. To be sure, Luke does understand Jesus as the heir of David's royal role as Son, in the sense of Psalm 2:7. The acclamation of Jesus as God's Son includes this kingly role, but something greater is here.[20] For Jesus' origins are mysteriously divine, and his personal identity is closely bound with God's own being in a way that transcends the God-relation of any of Israel's past kings or prophets.

Jesus as the awaited LORD *of the new exodus.* Beyond the passages that identify Jesus as God's Son, we must consider also several texts in Luke's Gospel that ascribe to Jesus roles and actions that are reserved in Israel's

Scripture for God alone. Prominent among these are the passages that announce Jesus' saving activity in imagery drawn from the Isaianic proclamation of a new exodus. Luke's extended citation of Isaiah 40:3-5 functions as a programmatic introduction to the narrative of Jesus' ministry (Luke 3:4-6); it frames his activity in terms of Isaiah's visionary prophecy of the end of Israel's exile and thereby serves as a "hermeneutical key for the Lukan program."[21] Particularly significant is the fact that Luke concludes his citation of Isaiah 40 with the climactic declaration that "all flesh will see *the salvation of God*." What implications might this programmatic reference to a new exodus have for understanding Jesus' own identity? Or what might it mean to proclaim that in him "the salvation of our God" becomes visible? To that question we now turn.

In the original prophetic context, there is no question that "the way of the Lord" (דֶּרֶךְ יְהוָה; LXX: τὴν ὁδὸν κυρίου) in Isaiah 40:3 refers to the path through the wilderness of Israel's God, as shown by the following line, in synonymous parallelism: "Make straight in the desert a highway for our God." Luke's form of the citation, like Mark's, substitutes the pronoun αὐτοῦ for this explicit reference to God in the second line of the couplet: "Make straight *his* paths."[22] This has the effect of leaving "Lord" in the first line ambiguous: when Luke writes "prepare the way of the Lord," should the reader understand this as a reference to *God's* impending arrival or as an anticipation of the coming of *Jesus*, to whom the narrator has already referred at least twice as "Lord" (1:43; 2:11)?[23] Both readings are possible; indeed, as Kavin Rowe has demonstrated, the ambiguity actually serves Luke's narrative purpose of producing an "overlap" *or* "shared identity" between Jesus the κύριος and the κύριος of Israel.[24]

A similar ambiguity attends the earlier reference in Zechariah's prophecy about his son John: "For you will go before the Lord to prepare his ways" (1:76). The foregoing reference in Gabriel's announcement of John's birth (1:16-17) would predispose the reader to hear "Lord" as a reference to "the Lord God," but in fact as the plot of the story unfolds, we see that John's role is to be the forerunner of *Jesus*, to whom the narrator refers repeatedly as the κύριος. This role of John as Jesus' predecessor is underscored once again in 7:24-30, this time through the citation of Malachi 3:1 / Exodus 23:20: "This is the one about whom it is written, 'Look, I am sending my messenger before your face, who will prepare your way before you'" (v. 27). In the narrative context of Luke 7, there can be no doubt that the point of the citation is to affirm that John was sent before *Jesus* to prepare *his* way.

The most significant observation here is that in Luke 3:1-6, Luke has taken the keynote passage from Isaiah 40 that declares the salvific coming of Israel's God and worked it narratively into an announcement of the imminent coming of Jesus as the one who would bring "the salvation of God" (3:6, citing Isa 40:5 LXX). Luke's citation of the extended block of material from Isaiah 40:3-5 strongly suggests that he is aware of the full context of Isaiah 40. If so, this identification of Jesus as the one in whom "all flesh will see the salvation of God" is hermeneutically momentous, for it is precisely in Isaiah 40 that we find one of the most radical declarations in all of Scripture of the *incomparability* of God:

> To whom, then, will you compare me,
> or who is my equal? says the Holy One. (Isa 40:25)

It is precisely because God alone possesses all sovereign power that the nations are "like a drop from a bucket" before him (40:15); that is why he, and he alone, can promise to rescue Israel from captivity. Isaiah's announcement of the new exodus is predicated on the bold claim that the all-powerful God is coming to save his people:

> Get you up to a high mountain,
> O herald of good tidings to Zion;
> lift up your voice with strength,
> O herald of good tidings to Jerusalem,
> lift it up, do not fear;
> say to the cities of Judah,
> "Here is your God!"
> *See, the Lord God* [LXX: κύριος] *comes* with might,
> and his arm rules for him. (Isa 40:9-10a, NRSV alt. transl.)

Thus, when Luke 3:4-6 draws on Isaiah 40 to intimate that Jesus is the coming κύριος of whom John speaks, the one whose glorious salvation will be for all flesh, the linkage between this coming figure and the Holy One of Israel can hardly be incidental.[25]

Jesus as Kyrios. But what is at stake in the identification of Jesus as κύριος? Luke is the only one of the Gospel writers who regularly uses κύριος as a title for Jesus. Κύριος is, of course, the Greek word used by the Septuagint to translate the holy name of God, the Tetragrammaton.

And Luke regularly follows this usage. For a particularly clear example, see Luke 1:16: "He will turn many of the people of Israel to *the Lord* their God." And yet there are also at least fifteen instances in Luke's Gospel where the Evangelist refers to Jesus as the κύριος—many of them in his own authorial voice.[26] Consider the following examples: "And why has this happened to me, that the mother of *my Lord* comes to me?" (Luke 1:43); "to you is born this day in the city of David a Savior, who is Christ *the Lord*" (2:11 RSV); "when *the Lord* saw her, he had compassion for her" (7:13); "John summoned two of his disciples and sent them to *the Lord* to ask . . ." (7:18b-19a); "Mary, who sat at *the Lord*'s feet" (10:39); "*The Lord* turned and looked at Peter" (22:61); "*The Lord* has risen indeed" (24:34). In short, Luke *in his own narration* quite remarkably applies the title κύριος both to the God of Israel and to Jesus of Nazareth—occasionally in a way that suggests a mysterious fusion of divine and human identity in the figure of Jesus.[27] This is not a result of editorial carelessness. Luke has deployed his references to Jesus as κύριος with careful compositional skill to shape the reader's understanding of Jesus' divine identity.[28]

The culmination of Luke's references to Jesus as κύριος appears in chapter 10 of Acts, in Peter's address to the Roman centurion Cornelius and his household: "[God] sent the word to the sons of Israel by proclaiming the gospel of peace through Jesus Christ; this one is Lord of all [πάντων κύριος]" (Acts 10:36).[29] This programmatic declaration about Jesus' identity is doubly startling. For the Roman centurion, Peter's ascription of the title "Lord of all" to Jesus can only be heard as a frontal challenge to the imperial propaganda that assigns exactly this honor of universal lordship to Caesar. For example, an imperial inscription from the time of Nero refers to him as ὁ τοῦ παντὸς κόσμου κύριος Νέρων.[30] And Epictetus wryly puts into the mouth of his interlocutor the boast, "But who can put me under compulsion except Caesar, the lord of all [ὁ παντῶν κύριος]?"[31] But at the same time, in a Jewish scriptural context, there is one and only one who can be acclaimed as "Lord of all." The fundamental Deuteronomic confession of Israel's faith declares that there can be only one Lord: ἄκουε Ισραηλ κύριος ὁ θεὸς ἡμῶν κύριος εἷς ἐστιν (Deut 6:4).

Thus, the hermeneutical effect of Luke's repeated description of Jesus as κύριος is not unlike the effect achieved at the end of Paul's Christ-hymn in Philippians 2, which astonishingly ascribes to Jesus the eschatological Lordship that Isaiah 45:23 emphatically reserves for God alone: "so that at the name of Jesus every knee should bend . . . and every tongue should confess that Jesus Christ is *Kyrios*, to the glory of God the Father" (Phil 2:10-11). In that same confession, Luke invites his readers to join.

Reception and rejection of the divine visitation. Once we see this pattern of christological claims taking shape in Luke's Gospel, we can go back through the text and perceive, on a second reading, that a Christology of divine identity also illumines and integrates numerous other details in Luke's picture that would otherwise seem incongruous or, at best, random.

In several passages, Luke tells the story in a way that creates a fusion of Jesus' activity with God's. The clearest example appears in Luke's version of the ending of the Gerasene demoniac story (Luke 8:39). Jesus instructs him, "Go back to your house and narrate how much *God* has done for you [ὅσα σοι ἐποίησεν ὁ θεός]." Luke then wraps up the story this way: "And he went away proclaiming through the whole city how much *Jesus* had done for him [ὅσα ἐποίησεν αὐτῷ ὁ Ἰησοῦς]." The parallelism is hardly accidental, and Luke offers no hint that the man's proclamation is either erroneous or disobedient; rather, the reader is left to infer that what Jesus had done *was* in fact what God had done. Similar instances show up several times subsequently in the story. For example, immediately following the transfiguration, Jesus heals a demon-afflicted boy and gives him back to his father. Luke concludes the episode by remarking, "And all were astounded at the greatness of *God*" (9:43). And again, in Luke's distinctive story of the healing of ten lepers (17:11-19), the one leper who turns back is described as first glorifying God, then falling on his face at Jesus' feet and giving thanks to him—a thoroughly understandable response in the narrative context. The subtle and interesting twist, however, occurs in Jesus' own commentary on the event, which seems to be either a musing to himself or a rhetorical aside addressed to the reader: "Were not the ten cleansed? But where are the nine? Were none of them found returning to give glory *to God* except this foreigner?" (17:17-18). Somehow the leper's action of returning to give thanks to Jesus is closely bound together with—or even identified with—giving praise and glory to God.[32] Taken by themselves, these examples do not prove anything about Jesus' direct identity with God. But read in the context of the other passages we have considered, they are suggestive that something more is here than might meet the eye on a first reading.

Consider, for example, the way that Luke connects Jesus' mission with the OT theme of God's "visitation" of his people. The paradigmatic precursor text is the scene following the call of Moses in the book of Exodus (4:27-31). Moses and Aaron assemble the elders of the people; Aaron, the spokesman, explains what God has told Moses and performs signs in the sight of the people. Then, according to the LXX account, "the people believed and rejoiced, because God *visited* [ἐπισκέψατο] the sons of Israel, and because he saw their affliction; and the people bowed down and worshiped" (Exod 4:31).[33] It is against this background that we should understand the reaction of the crowd upon witnessing Jesus' raising of the dead son of the widow at Nain: "Great fear seized them all, and they glorified God, saying 'A great prophet has been raised up among us' and '*God has visited* [ἐπισκέψατο] *his people*'" (Luke 7:16). We are seeing here the narrative outworking of the saving event proleptically announced by Zechariah in the beginning of Luke's story: "God *has visited* [ἐπισκέψατο] *his people* and made redemption for them" (Luke 1:76).

Jesus' appearance and powerful acts of grace show that God has at last begun to answer the prayers of the psalmists—particularly in their Septuagintal form. For example, in Psalm 105:4 LXX (= Ps 106:4 MT), we hear this fervent prayer: "Remember us Lord, in the favor you have for your people; *visit us* with your salvation [ἐπίσκεψαι ἡμᾶς ἐν τῷ σωτηρίῳ σου]." Or again, in Psalm 79 LXX (= Ps 80 MT), an extended metaphor likens Israel to a vine that God has planted but now left to be consumed and destroyed by invading forces; the psalmist then offers up this appeal: "O God of mighty acts, turn then, look upon us from heaven and see and *visit* [ἐπίσκεψαι] this vine" (Ps 79:15 LXX). Both of these Psalms recall God's deliverance of Israel from Egypt and intercede for a similar renewal of God's saving mercy, in which God will hear the cry of the people and come ("visit") to save them again.[34]

This same framework of expectation also informs Zechariah's prophetic hope that "through the tender mercy of our God . . . the dawn [ἀνατολή] from on high will *visit* [ἐπισκέψεται] us" (Luke 1:78). The image of the *Anatolē* (a word that can mean either "dawn" or, less commonly, "branch") is attested in Jewish sources as a designation for a new messianic Davidic ruler (as in Zech 3:8; 6:12). Yet the hope that this *Anatolē* will come "from on high" suggests that the desired coming Messiah may have a heavenly, more than merely human, origin.[35] And Luke's choice

of the verb ἐπισκέψεται in Luke 1:78 re-echoes the message of 1:76 that
God is the one who will visit and redeem. Thus, Luke leads the reader to
perceive that John's vocation to "go before the face of *the Lord* to prepare
his way" (1:76) will in fact portend the coming and *visitation* not of some
intermediary but of none other than Israel's God.

But there is also an ominous note in the announcement of God's visitation, for as the plot of the Gospel unfolds not all in Israel acknowledge and
welcome Jesus as the one who brings deliverance. That is why, when Jesus
at last draws near to Jerusalem, he weeps over it and prophesies its destruction, "because you did not recognize the time of your *visitation* [τὸν καιρὸν
τῆς ἐπισκοπῆς σου]" (19:44). The weeping figure in this scene is not merely
a distraught prophet who, like Elisha in 2 Kings 8:11-12, foresees a coming
catastrophe to be inflicted on Israel; instead, he is the one in whom God's
saving visitation is personally enacted. His tears anticipate the rejection
that he will suffer at the hands of his own people precisely because they fail
to recognize his true identity as the one in whom God is present to them.

The same motif of rejection of the divine presence is subtly foreshadowed in Luke's earlier account of Jesus' healing of a crippled, bent-over
woman (13:10-17). Jesus declares her to be a "daughter of Abraham" who
has long been bound by Satan but now "loosed from this bondage on the
day of the sabbath." As God liberated Israel from bondage in Egypt, so
Jesus' liberating act of healing is a sign of God's renewed liberation of his
people. But this act of sabbath liberation is opposed by the leader of the
synagogue, who seeks to turn the crowd against Jesus (13:14). After Jesus'
decisive reply in verses 15-16 (once again here Luke describes him tellingly as ὁ κύριος), his detractors back down. The language in which Luke
describes their silencing contains a subliminal echo of Isaiah 45:16 LXX:

> Luke 13:17a: καὶ ταῦτα λέγοντος αὐτοῦ κατῃσχύνοντο πάντες οἱ
> ἀντικείμενοι αὐτῷ.
> And when he said this, *all those who oppose him were put to shame.*
> Isa 45:16a LXX: αἰσχυνθήσονται καὶ ἐντραπήσονται πάντες οἱ
> ἀντικείμενοι αὐτῷ.
> *All those who oppose him shall be put to shame* and disgraced.

If we are justified in hearing this echo, its metaleptic force is considerable
in the Lukan narrative.[36] Consider the wider context of the passage in the
LXX, which differs here noticeably from the MT:

For you are God, and we did not know you, the God of Israel, the Savior.
All those who oppose him shall be put to shame and disgraced, and shall
walk in shame. You islands, dedicate yourselves to me. Israel is saved by
the Lord with an everlasting salvation; forevermore, they shall not be
ashamed nor disgraced. (Isa 45:15-17 LXX)

The note explicitly sounded by Luke is the shaming of Jesus' opponents,
just as the prophecy of Isaiah foretells that those who oppose the God of
Israel will be shamed. But the implicit overtones of the echo also whisper
that the κύριος Jesus *is* the God of Israel, the Savior (cf. Luke 2:11), whom
these opponents have failed to know. The islands (a frequent Isaian locu-
tion for the wider Gentile world) will in due course dedicate themselves to
him, and Israel—or at least those in Israel who do come to know him will
indeed receive the promise of everlasting salvation, as symbolized by the
liberation of the daughter of Abraham in Luke's story. Thus, if we hear
the echo of Isaiah 45 LXX in Luke 13:10-17, we will see that this brief
narrative unit hints at Luke's larger plotline *in nuce*.

Jesus as object of worship. Another indicator of Jesus' divine identity is
found in the motif of Jesus as the object of worship. Luke, unlike Matthew, is notably restrained in his use of the verb προσκυνεῖν.[37] He reserves
all reference to the worship of Jesus until the very ending of his Gospel,
where we are told that the risen Jesus was carried up into heaven and that
the disciples "worshiped him [προσκυνήσαντες αὐτόν] and returned into
Jerusalem with great joy" (24:52). The narrative impact of this concluding
description is enhanced by the complete absence of other references to
"worship" in this story, save one: in the account of Jesus' temptation in the
wilderness, the devil seeks to cajole Jesus into worshiping him, and Jesus
emphatically rejects the temptation with a word of Scripture: "It is written, 'The Lord your God you will worship [προσκυνήσεις], and him alone
you will serve'" (4:8, quoting Deut 6:13). Given this single decisive directive, what are we to make of Luke's ending? It seems there are really only
three possibilities: the disciples' worship of the risen Jesus is a misguided
act of idolatry, or Jesus is in fact the Lord God, or Luke is a confused narrator.[38] It seems that the Gospel of Luke presses us incessantly toward the
second of these options.[39]

Jesus desires to gather Jerusalem under his wings. That is perhaps why, at
a couple of junctures in the narrative, Luke's Jesus disconcertingly speaks
as though from the divine perspective. The most striking example of this

dramatic device appears in Jesus' lament, in the midst of his journey to Jerusalem, over the city in which he knows he will perish: "Jerusalem, Jerusalem, the city that kills the prophets and stones those who are sent to her: how often I have desired to gather your children together as a bird gathers her brood under her wings, and you were not willing" (13:34).[40] This image derives its particular poignancy from its resonance with several OT passages in which Israel's God is depicted metaphorically as a bird spreading its wings to protect Israel. In Deuteronomy 32:10-12, God's care for Israel (here personified as "Jacob") in the wilderness is compared to an eagle's care for its young:

> He sustained him in a desert land,
> in a howling wilderness waste;
> he shielded him, cared for him,
> guarded him as the apple of his eye.
> *As an eagle stirs up its nest,*
> *and hovers over its young;*
> *as it spreads its wings, takes them up,*
> *and bears them aloft on its pinions,*
> the LORD alone guided him;
> no foreign god was with him.

A similar image appears in Psalm 91, in the psalmist's confident expression of trust in God as Israel's refuge:

> You who live in the shelter of the Most High,
> who abide in the shadow of the Almighty,
> will say to the LORD, "My refuge and my fortress;
> my God, in whom I trust."
> For he will deliver you from the snare of the fowler
> and from the deadly pestilence;
> *he will cover you with his pinions,*
> *and under his wings you will find refuge.* (Ps 91:1-4a)

With images such as these shaping Israel's understanding of God's providential care,[41] the hearer of Jesus' lament in Luke 13:34 will immediately be struck by two remarkable features of his sorrowful words. First, even though Jesus is facing impending violence and death, he does not appeal to God to grant the protection of sheltering wings; instead, he casts himself, at least metaphorically, in the role of the God whose wings seek to shelter Jerusalem. Second, his lament portrays Jerusalem as rejecting the protection he has repeatedly sought to give (even though Luke's narrative makes no mention of any previous visits by Jesus to Jerusalem!), just as Israel in Deuteronomy 32 is portrayed as a stubborn people who have forgotten the God who gave them birth (Deut 32:15-18). Who then should we understand to be the speaker in Luke 13:34? Who is it that wishes to have gathered Jerusalem under his wings? These daring words can hardly be merely the complaint of a rejected prophet. They are nothing other than a cry from the heart of Israel's God.[42]

A slightly less dramatic example of Jesus' speech in the persona of God appears in Luke's apocalyptic discourse, in which Jesus warns his disciples of coming persecution and admonishes them not to worry ahead of time about how to speak to the kings and governors who will arrest them. Why? Because, he assures them, "I will give you a mouth and a wisdom that none of those who oppose you will be able to stand against or contradict" (21:14-15). Since Jesus has already prophesied his own impending death, this word of assurance seems to presuppose not only his continuing power beyond death to aid his followers but also his authority to confer speech and wisdom in a supernatural manner, just as God promised to give Moses the words to speak before Pharaoh: "Who gives speech to mortals? Who makes them mute or deaf, seeing or blind? Is it not I, the Lord? Now go, I will be with your mouth and teach you what you are to speak" (Exod 4:11-12).[43]

The authority claimed here for Jesus belongs to a larger pattern of Lukan narration in which Jesus is said to confer powers and blessings that no one but God could confer. How is it that he can appoint disciples and give them authority over demons and diseases (Luke 9:1-2; 10:19)? How can he promise, after the resurrection, to send power from on high ("the promise of the Father") upon his followers (24:49) and then, in the dramatic opening scenes of Acts, fulfill that promise by pouring out the Holy Spirit (Acts 2:33)? Even more than the power to forgive sins or still storms, surely the power to send the Spirit is a prerogative that belongs exclusively to God.[44] In Peter's Pentecost sermon, the solution to this riddle is made clear: the outpouring of God's Spirit demonstrates that the risen Jesus is seated at God's right hand where he possesses the divine authority that was prefigured in the mysterious words of Psalm 110:1. Simply put, Jesus has the authority to send the Spirit because, as David declared long ago, he is "Lord." The Spirit that Jesus now sends is the

same Spirit that God named as "my Spirit" in the prophecy of Joel 3:1
(= ET 2:28) and promised to pour out on all flesh (Acts 2:17). While the
relations here between Father, Son, and Spirit are complex (I will forbear
from any attempt to situate Luke's position in relation to the later controversy over the *filioque* clause!), we see that in the giving of the Spirit there
is once again the closest possible *Verbindung* of Jesus' identity with the
divine identity.

The One Who Redeems Israel

In view of these exegetical observations, I would hazard the following
conclusion: *the "low" Christology that modern NT criticism has perceived in
Luke's Gospel is an artificial construction that can be achieved only by ignor-
ing—or suppressing—the hermeneutical relevance of the powerful Old Testament allusions in Luke's story. It is therefore precisely by attending more fully
to the Old Testament intertexts in Luke's Gospel that we gain a deeper and
firmer grasp of the theological coherence between Luke's narrative testimony
and what the church's dogmatic tradition has classically affirmed about the
identity of Jesus.*

It is perhaps also noteworthy that Luke omits or transforms some of
the "non-divine-identity" material from his Markan source. The saying
about Jesus' ignorance of the day and hour of the eschatological events
(Mark 13:32 / Matt 24:38) finds no parallel in Luke, and Luke famously
replaces Jesus' cry of dereliction with a decisive and gracious act of com-
mending his spirit into God's hands—replacing the cry of Psalm 22:1
with a citation of Psalm 31:5 and thereby avoiding the appearance of separation between Jesus and God. Luke does, of course, retain an abbre-
viated version of the scene of Jesus' agonized prayer in Gethsemane
(22:39-46). But on the whole, Luke's editorial reception and adaptation
of the Markan tradition has the effect of deleting or minimizing some of
the apparently "low" christological elements and, as we have seen, adding
significant new material to suggest Jesus' identity with the God of Israel.

We conclude these reflections on the identity of Jesus in Luke's
Gospel, then, by returning to Cleopas and his anonymous companion
on the road to Emmaus. "We had hoped," they say dejectedly, "that he
was the one who was going to redeem Israel [ὁ μέλλων λυτροῦσθαι τὸν
Ἰσραήλ]." We have seen throughout this essay that their hope, however

ill informed, was not wrong: the plaintive words of the Emmaus road trudgers point ironically and unerringly to the deepest truth about Jesus: he is the Redeemer of Israel. And who, according to the scriptural witness, is the Redeemer of Israel? The answer lies in a catena of texts from Isaiah. Let us read backwards and hear them afresh, recalling that the chief concern of the mysterious stranger on the road was to elucidate the ways in which "the things about himself" were imbedded in Scripture:

> Do not fear, you worm Jacob, you insect Israel!
> I will help you, says the LORD;
> your Redeemer (LXX: ὁ λυτρούμενος) is the Holy One of Israel.
> (Isa 41:14)[45]

> Thus says the LORD,
> your Redeemer [LXX: ὁ λυτρούμενος], the Holy One of Israel:
> For your sake I will send to Babylon
> and break down all the bars,
> and the shouting of the Chaldeans will be turned to lamentation.
> I am the LORD, your Holy One,
> the Creator of Israel, your King. (Isa 43:14-15)

> Thus says the LORD, your Redeemer [LXX: ὁ λυτρούμενός σε],
> who formed you in the womb:
> I am the LORD, who made all things,
> who alone stretched out the heavens,
> who by myself spread out the earth;
> . . . who says of Jerusalem, "It shall be inhabited,"
> and of the cities of Judah, "They shall be rebuilt,
> and I will raise up their ruins." (Isa 44:24, 26b)

> Thus says the LORD,
> the Redeemer of Israel and his Holy One [LXX: ὁ ῥυσάμενός σε ὁ θεὸς
> Ἰσραήλ],
> to one deeply despised, abhorred by the nations,
> the slave of rulers,
> "Kings shall see and stand up,
> princes, and they shall prostrate themselves,
> because of the LORD, who is faithful,
> the Holy One of Israel, who has chosen you." (Isa 49:7)

The brilliant dramatic irony of Luke's Emmaus road scene nudges readers inexorably toward a subtle but overwhelming conclusion: the two disciples are wrong to be discouraged but right to have hoped for Jesus to be the one who would redeem Israel. In their puzzled disappointment, they truly name Jesus' identity without realizing what they are saying, for the Redeemer of Israel is none other than Israel's God. And Jesus, in truth, is the embodied, unrecognized, but scripturally attested presence of the One for whom they unwittingly hoped.

5

The Temple Transfigured

Reading Scripture with John

John's Use of Scripture: Overview

"We have found the one about whom Moses wrote in the Law, and also the prophets." In one of the opening scenes of John's Gospel, Jesus abruptly summons a man named Philip to follow him. Philip then seeks out his friend Nathanael and declares, without providing evidence or explanation, "We have found the one about whom Moses wrote in the Law, and also the prophets: Jesus, the son of Joseph from Nazareth" (John 1:45). Nathanael understandably expresses a certain sardonic skepticism: Can anything worthwhile come out of an insignificant village like Nazareth? Philip simply replies, "Come and see" (1:46).

That summons, "Come and see," functions also as an invitation to the reader of the Fourth Gospel, an invitation to discern, among other things, whether the Jesus they will meet in this story is in fact prefigured by Moses and the prophets. John has set astonishingly high expectations in the first chapter of his narrative: the opening paragraphs of the story already identify Jesus, a mysterious figure from a small Galilean village, as the *Logos* through whom creation came into being (1:1-18), as "the Lamb of God who takes away the sin of the world" (1:29-36), and as Israel's Messiah (1:41). And, for reasons opaque to the reader, Philip now identifies Jesus—who has not yet done anything, at least not anything reported by the narrator—as the true referent to whom Israel's Scriptures point, the Law and the prophets alike. It is of course possible that Philip has leaped to a false inference, that he has blurted out an exaggerated and misleading claim—as overeager followers often do. But the solemn opening of John's narrative suggests otherwise: we are given to understand that Philip has somehow intuited a revelatory insight. If so, readers of the text are summoned by Philip's words to come and see *how* this Jesus of Nazareth can be understood as the one about whom Moses and the prophets wrote. But Philip does not actually cite any texts; what passages in Moses and the prophets does he have in mind? And will Jesus accept this portentous description of his identity and somehow fulfill Philip's hermeneutical expectation? To find the answers, we must move deeper into the story.

As the plot unfolds, Jesus comes into conflict with religious authorities who charge him with violating the sabbath: Jesus has healed a lame man and instructed him to stand up and carry his mat (John 5:2-9). The offense lies not in the healing itself but in Jesus' directive to the man to carry his mat, an act that constitutes a technical violation of the commandment that prohibits working on the sabbath (John 5:10-16; cf. Exod 20:8-11; Deut 5:12-15).[1] But the argument quickly escalates from a halakhic dispute to a christological controversy when Jesus justifies his action by identifying his action with God's own: "But Jesus answered them, 'My Father is working even until now, and I also am working.' Therefore, the Jews sought all the more to kill him, because not only did he relax the sabbath law, but also he was calling God his own Father, thereby making himself equal with God" (John 5:17-18).

Their complaint then becomes the springboard for one of the long self-referential discourses of Jesus that are distinctively characteristic of the Fourth Gospel. And at the climax of this discourse, just about a quarter of the way through John's narrative, we come at last upon the fundamental hermeneutical claim—now stated in Jesus' own words—that illumines John's approach to reading Israel's Scripture. Jesus upbraids his detractors for failing to receive him as the one sent by God:

> "You search the Scriptures, because you think that in them you have eternal life; and *those very Scriptures are the ones that bear witness concerning me.* But you do not want to come to me in order that you might have life. . . . Do not think that I will accuse you before the Father. But there is one who accuses you: Moses, upon whom you have set your hope. *For if you believed Moses, you would believe me, for he wrote about me.* But if you do not believe the writings of Moses, how will you believe my words?"
> (5:39-40, 45-47)

So Philip was right. Jesus endorses Philip's eager description of him as "the one whom Moses wrote about in the Law." But there is a tragic turn: though Moses wrote about Jesus, the religious teachers of God's people, the ones whose office it is to explicate Moses, now find Jesus unbelievable and reject him. This bitter and paradoxical outcome was foreshadowed already in John's prologue: the Word "came to his own home, and his own people did not receive him" (1:11). But only here in John 5 does the *hermeneutical* dimension of this failure come fully into focus.

Jesus does not challenge or denigrate Moses; rather, Moses actually testifies to Jesus. Yet Jesus' adversaries, despite their earnest scrutiny of Moses' writings, lapse into interpretative failure because they reject Jesus' astonishing claim to be the true and ultimate referent to whom Moses' words point. There is a fateful circularity here: reading the writings of Moses should lead to believing in Jesus; but in order to understand Moses' words, one must first come to Jesus to receive life. "You do not have his word [τὸν λόγον αὐτοῦ] remaining in you, because the one he has sent, him you do not believe" (5:38). And so those who do not trust Jesus' word remain in incomprehension and death. Only those who enter this hermeneutical loop at the point of believing Jesus can rightly understand what Moses wrote.

And so in John's Gospel, just as in Luke's, there is a call for a retrospective rereading of Israel's Scripture, a *reading backwards* that reinterprets Scripture in light of a new revelation imparted *by* Jesus and focused *on* the person of Jesus himself. Though the narratives of Luke and John are worlds apart stylistically—not least because of John's *polemical* framing of his remarks about the testimony of Scripture—their hermeneutical underpinnings are similar, and the theological distance between Luke 24:27 and John 5:46 is even less than the mere five chapters that would ultimately separate them in the church's fourfold Gospel canon.

> Luke 24:27: "Then beginning with Moses and all the prophets, he interpreted to them the things about himself in all the scriptures."
> John 5:46: "If you believed Moses, you would believe me, for he wrote about me."

Yet despite this convergence, John's way of handling the biblical texts differs markedly from anything we have seen in the Synoptic Gospels. Let us then consider, by way of overview, what sort of reading of Moses John performs and exemplifies.

John contains relatively few direct citations of the Old Testament. C. K. Barrett long ago illustrated this fact simply by counting the references (including allusions) listed in the Westcott and Hort critical edition of the NT.[2] The totals are striking: Matthew, 124; Mark, 70; Luke, 109; John, 27. This counting may be slightly skewed, but it points to an undeniable feature of John's narrative. Just as he condenses the traditions of Jesus' healing and miracle-working activity down to a few selected episodes that are given more extended development than in the synoptic tradition, so also John focuses on a smaller number of OT quotations. Depending on the criteria employed, studies of John's use of the OT have identified between thirteen and seventeen explicit quotations.[3] Precisely because there are relatively few quotations, each citation that does appear in John's uncluttered narrative assumes proportionately greater gravity as a pointer to Jesus' identity. If Luke is the master of the deft, fleeting allusion, John is the master of the carefully framed, luminous image that shines brilliantly against a dark canvas and lingers in the imagination. (In this respect, John's narrative technique is analogous to the visual artistry of Rembrandt's portraits.) John is not attempting to compile the maximum number of illustrations of how Moses wrote about Jesus. He knows that much more could be said (cf. 21:25), but he prefers to focus on the artistically selected instance that repays sustained meditation.

That is why, in addition to the smaller number of quotations, there is also a surprisingly low number of obvious verbal allusions to Israel's Scripture in John's Gospel.[4] Or, to put the point more precisely, John's manner of alluding does not depend upon the citation of chains of words and phrases; instead it relies upon evoking *images* and *figures* from Israel's Scripture. For example, when he writes, "And just as Moses lifted up the serpent in the wilderness, so it is necessary for the Son of Man to be lifted up" (3:14), John is clearly alluding to the episode narrated in Numbers 21:8-9, but the only explicit *verbal* links between the two passages are the name "Moses" and the word "serpent" (ὄφιν).[5] His intertextual sensibility is more visual than auditory.

To be sure, John does also deal in verbal echoes. The best-known instance is the Gospel's opening sentence, "In the beginning was the Word," which both echoes and transforms Genesis 1:1. This is just one of many examples in John's text, some of them very subtle. For example, in John's allusion to Moses and the bronze serpent, the verb "lifted up" (ὕψωσεν/ὑψωθῆναι), which appears nowhere in Numbers 21, may well echo the introductory lines of Isaiah's description of the mysterious suffering servant: "Behold, my servant will understand, and will be lifted up [ὑψωθήσεται] and will be glorified exceedingly" (Isa 52:13 LXX). These echoes of Numbers and Isaiah are verbally faint (echoing just a word or two from the scriptural source) but symbolically potent, evoking a rich theological matrix within which the Fourth Gospel's presentation of Jesus is to be understood.

However, John also introduces a substantial number of direct quotations with explicit quotation formulas, often in the form of authorial commentary—in this way resembling Matthew more than Mark or Luke. These formulas follow a pattern that mirrors the structural design of the narrative. From the beginning of the story up until almost the end of chapter 12—that is, throughout the account of Jesus' active public ministry, sometimes designated "the book of signs"—John introduces quotations with "as it is written," "it is written in the prophets," "as Scripture said," or some minor variation on these phrasings (1:23; 2:17; 6:31; 6:45; 7:38; 7:42; 10:34; 12:14). But after Jesus withdraws from public proclamation and activity (12:36b), there is a striking change. After this pivotal point in the plot, almost all the subsequent quotations are introduced with a fulfillment formula employing forms of πληρόω: "in order that the Scripture might be fulfilled," or slight variation.[6]

The only exceptions appear in 12:39 ("because again Isaiah said") and 19:37 ("and again another Scripture says"). In both of these instances, the quotation introduced is the second of a pair, as signaled by πάλιν ("again"). It is hardly accidental that these pairs of linked quotations (12:38-40; 19:36-37) serve as end punctuation to the two central narrative blocks of the Gospel, the "book of signs" (1:19–12:50) and the "book of the passion" (13:1–19:42).[7] Like the closing cadence at the end of a movement in a symphony, these double fulfillment citations signal that a section of the story is drawing to a close.[8]

What is the significance of this change in the wording of scriptural citation formulas in the latter part of the Gospel? The overall stylistic and theological unity of the Fourth Gospel tells against a simple source-critical explanation; whatever sources may have been employed by the author of this carefully crafted text, he has shaped them into an artistic unity. It is unlikely that a feature as prominent as these fulfillment quotations could have been spliced into the narrative without the author's editorial reflection about the specific wording used to introduce them.

The likeliest explanation for the strong emphasis on "fulfillment" in the latter part of the Gospel is that these citations provide John's theological response to the otherwise incomprehensible adversity that Jesus encounters. The "book of signs" culminates in a grim reflection on the unbelief of the Jewish people in response to Jesus: "But although he did so many signs in their presence they persistently did not believe in him" (12:37; cf. 1:11).[9] This sad observation ruefully sums up the outcome of Jesus' public career and functions as a watershed point in the plot. John's shift thereafter to "fulfillment" language in his introductory formulas in the "book of the passion" signals an *apologetic* motivation: the Evangelist is explaining that the suffering and rejection experienced by Jesus in the passion story was not some unforeseen disaster; rather, it was foreordained and played out in fulfillment of God's will, with Jesus' full knowledge and participation.[10] The point may be demonstrated by a list of the events that are said to have happened "in order that the Scripture might be fulfilled."

> 12:37-40: They did not believe in him (Isa 53:1; 6:10).
>
> 13:18: One of the disciples will betray Jesus (Ps 41:9).
>
> 15:24-25: The world has seen and hated both Jesus and his Father (Pss 35:19; 69:5).
>
> 17:12: One disciple was destined to be lost (Ps 41:9?).
>
> 19:23-24: Soldiers divided Jesus' garments and cast lots for his tunic (Ps 22:19).
>
> 19:28-29: On the cross, Jesus said, "I thirst" and was offered vinegar to drink (Ps 69:21).
>
> 19:36-37: In the crucifixion, Jesus' legs were not broken (Exod 12:10, 46; Num 9:12; or Ps 34:21), but his side was pierced (Zech 12:10).

All these events are interpreted, with the aid of the scriptural citations, as the consummation of a divine design that is fully enacted in Jesus' death (19:30: τετέλεσται, "it has been brought to completion"). This apologetic motivation also explains why the fulfillment quotations in the Fourth

Gospel are clustered toward the end of the story rather than, as in Matthew, at the beginning.[11]

Margaret Daly-Denton has drawn attention to the heavy concentration of Psalm texts within the group of Old Testament passages cited by John. By her reckoning, more than 60 percent of John's quotations come from the Psalter.[12] Even if this number is slightly inflated, there can be no mistaking the prominence of Psalm passages in the intertextual "genetic code" of the Fourth Gospel. This emphasis on the Psalter follows almost inevitably from John's concentration on the passion and death of Jesus as the center of gravity in his narrative. Because the Psalms foreshadow—or, as John might prefer, express—the suffering of the crucified/exalted Jesus, it is understandable that a retrospective reading of Scripture as witness to Jesus would be drawn to these texts.[13] It is, however, curious that a Gospel which asserts that *Moses* wrote about Jesus would make so little effort to explicate the Pentateuch as christological prophecy. Of John's explicit quotations, only one (19:36) can plausibly be ascribed to the five books of Moses (the instruction not to break any of the bones of the Passover lamb [Exod 12:46; Num 9:12]), and even in this case the wording of John's citation is actually closer to Psalm 34:20 than to the directive given in Exodus 12, suggesting that even here "Moses" has been mediated—or filtered—through the Psalter.[14] This observation about John's explicit OT citations should give us some pause and lead us to look carefully elsewhere in the narrative for subtler traces of evidence that might support the curious claim of the Johannine Jesus that Moses "wrote about me" (5:46).

A key hermeneutical test case is the lapidary statement near the end of the Gospel's prologue: "The Law was given through Moses; grace and truth came through Jesus Christ" (1:17). How are these two clauses related to one another? Does the Law given through Moses point to the grace and truth of Jesus Christ (as 5:46 indicates), so that the latter confirms and completes the testimony of the former? Or does the grace and truth of Jesus Christ negate and supplant the Law?[15] This question hovers over the Gospel as a whole.

And as it hovers, readers may wonder at numerous points whether John's story is supersessionist: Does it declare Judaism null and void and replace it with a new and different religion, Christianity, in which Israel's Law and Israel's hopes have been radically supplanted by an ethereal non-Jewish Christ who descends briefly from heaven into the world to reveal himself and then ascends again to a state of blessed detachment from the world? This way of formulating the problem already implies the answer that I think John's Gospel compels us to give: No. If we attend to the way that Scripture actually functions in John, we will see that the identity of Jesus is deeply imbedded in Israel's texts and traditions—especially the traditions centered on the Temple and Israel's annual feasts. This is the world in which John's imagination is immersed; it is impossible to understand John's Jesus apart from the story of Israel and the liturgical festivals and symbols that recall and re-present that story. It is not accurate, then, to say that Jesus nullifies or replaces Israel's Torah and Israel's worship life. Rather, he *assumes* and *transforms* them. But to grasp the way in which this transformation works, we must enter more deeply into John's practices of figural reading. At the heart of John's figural world are two breathtaking imaginative discernments.

For John, Jesus becomes, in effect, the Temple. John writes his Gospel ten or twenty years after the great Temple in Jerusalem has been destroyed by the Romans. But in place of Herod's once-impressive stone building, now in ruins, John declares that Jesus' *body* is now the place where God dwells, the place where atonement for sin occurs, the place where the division between God and humanity is overcome.[16] He makes this extraordinary claim not by rejecting Israel's Scripture but by *rereading* it to show how it points, if we understand it rightly, to Jesus.

For John, Jesus is not only the Temple—the place where we meet God—but he is also himself the God who meets us and rescues us by gathering us into union with him. And the astonishing divine identity Christology of the Fourth Gospel, which declares the oneness of the Son with the Father, comes to expression precisely through John's exposition of Scriptural texts and images. So let us now turn to consider more closely in what ways John believed Moses to have written about Jesus.

Israel's Scriptures as Figural Matrix
for John's Christology

Jesus as Word and Wisdom (John 1:1-18). The opening words of John's Gospel echo the first words of Israel's Scripture: "In the beginning . . ." Although the echo consists of only two words (ἐν ἀρχῇ), its volume is amplified by the placement of these words at the outset of the narrative, corresponding to their placement as the opening words of Genesis. Even more significantly, John's prologue continues to evoke creation themes (John 1:3, 10) and images (light/darkness [1:4-5, 7-9; cf. Gen 1:3-5]). A reader conversant with Genesis could hardly fail to hear the echo, as the history of interpretation of John amply demonstrates. And as the prologue unfolds, the reader gradually learns that the mysterious *Logos* who was there "in the beginning" has become flesh and is to be identified directly with Jesus Christ (John 1:14-18). Thus, the effect of John's introduction is to identify Jesus as a figure present with (or one with) God in the primal act of creation: "All things came into being through him, and without him not one thing came into being" (John 1:3).

This is an astounding claim to make about a human being, a figure of the author's recent historical past. To be sure, the role here ascribed to the *Logos* is not without biblical precedent. Israel's scriptural tradition contains several significant references to a preexistent figure of Wisdom as participant in the creation of the world, most notably in Proverbs 8:22-31. Although Wisdom (חָכְמָה, σοφία) is said to have been created (LXX: κύριος ἔκτισέν με) or, as the Hebrew text has it, "acquired" (קָנָנִי) at the beginning of God's works or ways (Prov 8:22), she is described as present with God "before the beginning of the earth" and beside God as a "master worker" (אָמוֹן) in the formation of the world.[17] In its original context in Proverbs, this language is almost surely to be understood as poetic personification of God's attibute of wisdom rather than as description of an actual quasi-divine *hypostasis*. It is not difficult to see, however, how over time the figure of personified Wisdom could develop into a mythologically conceived personage; indeed, we already see hints of this development in Wisdom of Solomon (see especially Wisdom 10), though the chief tendency of many later Jewish texts is to identify the figure of Wisdom as a personification of Torah (as in Sir 24:1-23 and Bar 3:35–4:4).

In the writings of Philo, we see that this quasi-personified role of mediation between God and the creation is assigned explicitly not to a feminine figure of *Sophia* but instead now to the figure of the *Logos*, as in the famous passage from *Quis rerum divinarum heres sit*, 205–6:

> To his *Logos*, His chief messenger, highest in age and honour, the Father of all has given the special prerogative to stand on the border and separate the creature from the Creator. This same *Logos* both pleads with immortal [God] as suppliant for afflicted mortality and acts as ambassador of

the Ruler to the subject.... [He is] neither uncreated by God, nor created as you, but midway between the two extremes, a surety to both sides.[18]

In Philo, all this seems to have the character of philosophical speculation. The *Logos* for Philo, even if quasi-personified, is a figurative and certainly noncorporeal entity that symbolizes something like God's creative power of reason. But John, in his prologue (1:1-18), astonishingly claims that the *Logos* became *flesh*.

The prologue of John's Gospel is best understood as a midrash on Genesis 1, a midrash that links the idea of a preexistent creative divine *Logos* to the motif of divine Wisdom seeking a home in the world (e.g., Sir 24:3-8). In contrast, however, to those earlier Jewish traditions that identify the earthly presence of Wisdom among the people Israel or in Israel's Law (Sir 24:23; Bar 3:35–4:4), John insists that *Logos*/Wisdom found only rejection in the world, even among God's own people.

> He was in the world, and the world came into being through him; yet the world did not know him. He came to what was his own, and his own people did not accept him. (John 1:10-11)

This appears very similar to the rather gloomy account offered in 1 Enoch 42:

> Wisdom could not find a place in which she could dwell; but a place was found for her in the heavens. Then Wisdom went out to dwell with the children of the people, but she found no dwelling place. So Wisdom returned to her place and she settled permanently among the angels. (1 Enoch 42:1-2)

But the Gospel of John offers a radically different conclusion to this unhappy story. Rather than taking up permanent residence among the angels, the divine Word/Wisdom acted to overcome Israel's resistance by becoming flesh in the person of Jesus: "And the Word became flesh and lived [ἐσκήνωσεν] among us, and we have seen his glory, the glory as of a father's only son, full of grace and truth" (1:14).[19] Thus, the prologue of the Fourth Gospel immediately situates Jesus in relation to Jewish scriptural traditions about *creation* and *Wisdom* while at the same time transforming those traditions through the startling claim that the Word/Wisdom through whom everything was made has become enfleshed in Jesus.[20]

This remarkable assertion in turn carries wide-ranging hermeneutical implications for the way that John *reads backwards* to reinterpret Israel's

Scripture and Israel's worship traditions: he asserts that Jesus, as the incarnation of God's Word, takes up into himself the significance of the Temple and its cycle of liturgical festivals. One of the clearest expressions of this hermeneutical device appears near the beginning of the narrative, after Jesus has driven the sellers and moneychangers out of the Temple. This passage gives us a crucial point of entry to the scriptural matrix within which we must read John's story of Jesus.

Remembering Scripture and Jesus' word (2:13-22). John emplots his distinctive account of Jesus' dramatic protest against the merchants and moneychangers in the Temple near the beginning of his narrative (2:13-22). The placement of the story is freighted with symbolic significance in two ways: (1) it foreshadows the conflict that leads to Jesus' passion and death (signaled by the quotation of Psalm 69:9: "Zeal for your house will consume me" [John 2:17]),[21] and (2) it points to the figural identification of Jesus' body as a *temple* that will be raised up in the resurrection (signaled by Jesus' own riddling words: "Destroy this temple, and in three days I will raise it up").

John presents both the scriptural text and the word of Jesus as enigmas that become comprehensible only *retrospectively*, only after the resurrection.[22] His emphasis on hermeneutical hindsight is highlighted by the parallelism between verses 17 and 22:

17: His disciples remembered that it was written. . . .
22: [H]is disciples remembered that he had said this. . . .

The Greek text in the two formulations is identical: ἐμνήσθησαν οἱ μαθηταὶ αὐτοῦ ὅτι. In both cases, John tells us, the disciples' understanding came only later, only as they read backwards to interpret Jesus' actions and words in light of the paradigm-shattering event of his resurrection. That is the point made emphatically in verse 22: "His disciples remembered . . . and they believed *the Scripture* and *the word that Jesus had spoken.*" This is consistent with the Evangelist's overall perspective on the crucial significance of memory and retrospective reading. Later in John's Gospel, in Jesus' farewell discourses, we learn that the disciples' postresurrection remembering is to be aided by the Paraclete, the Holy Spirit, who will recall and interpret Jesus' words for the community (John 14:25-26; 16:12-15). Even more explicitly than the other Gospel writers, then, John champions *reading backwards* as an essential strategy for illuminating

Jesus' identity. Only by reading backwards, in light of the resurrection, under the guidance of the Spirit, can we understand both Israel's Scripture and Jesus' words.

On this kind of postresurrection reading, we learn, among other things, that Jesus himself is the speaker of Psalm 69, the praying voice who declares, "Zeal for your house will consume me." And that insight in turn opens the window on a fresh appropriation of the entire psalm—indeed, perhaps the entire Psalter—as a proleptic veiled revelation of the identity of Jesus.[23] To be sure, in order to read the Psalms this way, we must cultivate a figural imagination. And so when John tells us that Jesus "was speaking of the Temple of his body," a light goes on: the Evangelist, here in the opening chapters of his story, is teaching his readers how to read. He is teaching us to read *figurally*, teaching us to read Scripture *retrospectively*, in light of the resurrection. Only on such a reading does it make sense to see the Jerusalem Temple as *prefiguring* the truth now definitively embodied in the crucified and risen Jesus.[24]

Thus, John 2:13-22 is of great importance for at least three reasons: (1) we are informed here that right interpretation of Scripture and of the traditions about Jesus could be done only *retrospectively* after the resurrection; (2) John instructs his readers to read *figurally*; and (3) the link between the Temple and Jesus' body is made explicit, providing a hermeneutical key for John's symbolism throughout the narrative. Jesus now takes over the Temple's function as a place of mediation between God and human beings.[25]

The hermeneutical revelation offered in 2:21 casts light on Jesus' earlier enigmatic declaration to Nathanael: "Truly, truly, I say to you, you will see the heaven opened and the angels of God ascending and descending upon the Son of Man" (1:51). Jesus has become the nexus between heaven and earth, and thus he fulfills Jacob's naming of the place of his dream vision as *Bethel*: "This is none other than *the house of God*, and this is the gate of heaven" (Gen 28:17). That is also why he can later say to the Samaritan woman, "Woman, believe me, the hour is coming when you will worship the Father neither on this mountain nor in Jerusalem" (4:21). True worship is focused on the person of Jesus himself, who is both the way to the Father and the place where the presence of God is made known (14:6-7)—indeed, the place where the presence of God dwells.

Jesus as embodiment of Sukkoth and Passover. The same logic applies throughout the Fourth Gospel to Jesus' assumption and replacement of the significance of Israel's religious festivals. For example, the rituals of *Sukkoth* (the Festival of Booths or Tabernacles)[26] involved outpourings of water and the kindling of lights in the Temple (in reminiscence of Zech 14:7-8, where the images of continuous light and flowing water are linked to the observance of the Festival of Booths in vv. 16-19); therefore, when Jesus cries out[27] on the last day of the festival of Sukkoth, "Let anyone who is thirsty come to me, and let the one who believes in me drink" (John 7:37-38) and—on the same occasion—"I am the light of the world" (8:12), he is taking onto himself the symbolism of the occasion, claiming both to fulfill and to supplant it.

Or, let us consider another festival: *Passover* symbolism is particularly pervasive in John's Gospel, coming to a climax in the passion narrative, where Jesus' crucifixion takes place on the *day of preparation* for Passover (19:14), not on Passover itself as in the Synoptic Gospels. The effect of this chronological shift is to align Jesus' death with the slaughter of the Passover lambs, a point underscored when John tells the reader that the Roman soldiers did not break the legs of Jesus on the cross, thus allowing his death to fulfill the requirement for the preparation of the Passover lamb: "These things occurred so that scripture might be fulfilled, 'None of his bones shall be broken'" (19:36, alluding to Exod 12:46). Jesus, "the lamb of God" (1:29), embodies in his death the true signification of the Passover and exodus events.

The Good Shepherd at the Feast of Dedication (John 10:22-30). All of this is fairly familiar to readers of John. But now let us look in more detail at one more festival whose symbolic significance for John is perhaps less widely recognized: the Feast of Dedication. The key text is John 10:22-30. John writes: "At that time the festival of the Dedication took place in Jerusalem. It was winter, and Jesus was walking in the temple, in the portico of Solomon." It is easy for us to read right over this, but anyone in first-century Israel would immediately have perceived the symbolically fraught character of this setting. The Festival of Dedication (*Hanukkah*), celebrates the victory of the Maccabean revolt against the oppressive Syrian ruler Antiochus Ephiphanes IV. It recalled both the renewal of Temple worship and the institution of national independence, like the

American Fourth of July—or like, say, the celebration of the end of apart-heid and the freedom of the South African people.

But by Jesus' day, the political scene had shifted again. The indepen-dent Jewish kingdom established by the Maccabean revolt had not lasted long. In the time of Jesus, Judea was ruled by a Roman governor, Pon-tius Pilate, and the Jewish people were once again under the thumb of a foreign power. The celebration of Hanukkah—the Festival of Dedica-tion—under these circumstances would have been a time when the Jew-ish people looked back nostalgically to an era of past national glory and, more dangerously, looked forward in hope to Israel's future liberation.

It is on *this* occasion that John describes Jesus walking in the Temple—and not just in the Temple, but specifically in the Portico of *Solomon*. Sol-omon, of course, the son of David, was the king who had most gloriously extended the scope of the ancient Israelite monarchy. And many of the Jewish people were longing for a new "son of David," a messiah who would restore the kingdom to Israel.

So as Jesus walks in Solomon's Portico, what words will he speak against this symbolic backdrop? Will he proclaim himself the new Solo-mon, the new son of David, the King of Israel? Will he launch a new revolt against the occupying power? That is why the people ask the question they do: "How long will you keep us in suspense? If you are the Messiah, tell us plainly" (10:24).

In one sense, Jesus has already answered the crowd's question. Ear-lier in John 10 he declared, "I am the good shepherd" (vv. 11, 14). For the crowd assembled in the Portico of Solomon, the image of the "good shepherd" also carried clear *political* significance because of a passage they would have known well from the prophecies of Ezekiel 34. The prophet, speaking in the name of God, scolded the leaders of Israel for failing to care properly for God's flock: they were selfish and careless shepherds who had allowed the sheep to be abused and scattered. And then, near the end of the chapter, we find this:

> I will set up over them one shepherd, my servant David, and he shall feed them: he shall feed them and be their shepherd. And I, the LORD will be their God, and my servant David shall be prince among them; I, the LORD, have spoken. (Ezek 34:23-24)

It is no wonder, then, that Jesus excited messianic speculation by claiming to be the good shepherd. The "good shepherd" is not simply a consoler who promises to care for the souls of those who believe. Rather, Jesus is staking symbolic claim to be the new David, the restorer and ruler of Israel. But he has said all this in *figurative* language. And so the crowd presses him for a more explicit declaration of his candidacy for royal office.

But Jesus avoids giving a direct answer. He points simply to the works he has been doing, saying that these testify sufficiently to his identity. What works does he mean? John tells us, for example, that Jesus healed a man who had been blind from birth and miraculously fed a hungry crowd. His works are works of healing and feeding: precisely what the good shepherd of Ezekiel 34 promised to do for the flock. These concrete acts of goodness and mercy should be sufficient proof that he is who he says he is. The passage ends, then, with a word of promise: "No one will snatch them out of my hand." Why? Because, he declares, "I and the Father are one" (10:30 RSV).

And here Jesus claims something that no first-century Jew expected of a messiah: he is one with God. That is why he can make the extravagant promise that no one will be able to snatch the sheep away from him.

How can it be so? The promise is valid if and only if Jesus' claim to be one with the Father is also true. The sheep are safe in Jesus' hand only because no one can snatch them out of *God's* hand. And here we must once again recall Ezekiel 34: according to Ezekiel's prophecy, it is not only David who will be the shepherd of the sheep but also God himself:

> I myself will be the shepherd of my sheep, and I will make them lie down, says the Lord God. I will seek the lost, and I will bring back the strayed, and I will bind up the injured, and I will strengthen the weak, but the fat and the strong I will destroy. I will feed them with justice.
> (Ezek 34:15-16)

So, on that chilly winter day in the Temple, Jesus is not talking about politics as usual. He is promising the redemption of the world on the other side of death and resurrection. And in John's narrative world, that promise is valid only because Jesus is the truth to which the Festival of Dedication points, through a glass darkly: he is the personal presence of the God of Israel, come at last to rescue his people, to heal and bind up, to feed them with justice.

In light of this sort of figurative hermeneutic, the entirety of the OT becomes figurally available to illumine the identity of Jesus. It is not a matter of locating a few prooftexts that predict events in Jesus' life. Rather, *John sees Israel's Scripture as figurally transparent to the One who became incarnate in Jesus.*

Bread from heaven (John 6:22-59). Once this realization dawns upon us, we see that it is not just the Temple and the festivals that prefigure Jesus: for John, it is the whole narrative of God's gracious dealing with Israel. Consider, for example, the story of the manna in the wilderness: John insists that it prefigures Jesus, who is the true "bread from heaven" (6:31-33).

After Jesus' miraculous feeding of the multitude in John 6, John tells an amusing story of the crowd pursuing Jesus around the Sea of Tiberias. They ask, "What sign are you going to give us then, so that we may see it and believe you? . . . Our ancestors ate the manna in the wilderness; as it is written, 'He gave them bread from heaven to eat'" (vv. 30-31). *What sign are you going to give us?* Their question is strange, for just on the previous day Jesus had provided them with food no less remarkable than the manna in the wilderness. What further sign could they possibly need? Their odd question is a symptom of deeper failure to understand what they have already witnessed. As T. S. Eliot writes, "We had the experience but missed the meaning."[28] They are expecting Jesus to fit the job description of the new prophet like Moses, and so their preconceived categories prevent them from seeing what is right before their eyes.

And so Jesus sets them straight. And here we come to the heart of the matter: *Jesus is teaching his hearers how to read Scripture.* The crowd has the right text—they have linked Jesus' feeding of the multitude with Psalm 78:24, which renarrates Exodus 16, the story of the manna in the wilderness.[29] They have the right text but the wrong reading. They seem to think the story is about Moses as a charismatic wonder-worker. And so Jesus must explain: "Very truly, I tell you, it was not *Moses* who gave you the bread from heaven, but it is *my Father* who gives you the true bread from heaven" (v. 32). Jesus is simply teaching them basic exegesis: when the text says "he gave them bread from heaven to eat," the subject of the sentence is *God*, not Moses.

But notice that Jesus' instruction in how to read goes beyond this simple corrective. Not only is it God the Father who is the true giver, but

Jesus changes the tense of the verb from past to present and suggests that the manna must be interpreted as a *prefiguration* of another, truer bread still to come: "[I]t is my Father who *gives* you the *true bread from heaven*." Here is the paradigm shift: the manna story is not just about a past event in salvation history; rather, it points forward *figurally* to a different kind of bread altogether. Even though the manna was divinely given, it was still "the food that perishes" (another exegetical allusion: cf. Exod 16:19-21), and those who ate it still died (John 6:49). John is once again teaching his readers how to reread Israel's Scripture by reading backwards: Jesus reinterprets the manna story as pointing to *himself*, prefiguring himself. The fact that the noun ἄρτος is masculine allows John to craft the artful ambiguity of Jesus' words: the participle καταβαίνων can be construed either as attributive ("the bread of God is that which comes down from heaven") or as substantive ("the bread of God is the One who comes down from heaven"). We will surely be faithful readers of John's figural hermeneutic if we hear distinct overtones of the latter interpretation. That is the hidden meaning of his cryptic statement: "For the bread of God is the One that comes down from heaven and gives life to the world" (6:33).

In response to this, the crowd finally gets beyond the wrong questions and makes the right request: "Sir, give us this bread always" (v. 34). They are like the Samaritan woman a little earlier in the story who asked Jesus, "Sir, give me this water, so that I may never be thirsty" (4:15). And Jesus, no longer speaking cryptically, gives them a dramatic answer similar to the answer he gave her: "*I am* [ἐγώ εἰμι]—I am the bread of life. Whoever comes to me will never be hungry, and whoever believes in me will never be thirsty" (6:34-35).

So, *by giving himself bodily, Jesus gives life to the world.* Jesus himself is the true bread from heaven, the bread toward which Israel's desire—indeed, the desire of all humanity—should be directed; he is the true meaning of the manna story. Jesus, the one who came from heaven, is the giver of life, and only when we come to him will we be given the life that endures and overcomes death. According to John's Gospel, that is the true meaning of what Moses wrote.

———

We could go on illustrating John's figural hermeneutic in passage after passage, but we must stop. The reading strategy that John exemplifies in these texts allows him to articulate his extraordinary (and polemical) claim that all of Scripture actually bears witness to Jesus: "If you believed Moses, you would believe me, for he wrote about me" (John 5:46). Thus, even more comprehensively than the other Gospels, John understands the Old Testament as a vast matrix of symbols pointing to Jesus. In contrast to Luke's reading of Scripture as a plotted script showing the outworking of God's promises in time, John understands Scripture as a huge web of signifiers generated by the pretemporal eternal *Logos* as intimations of his truth and glory.

John reads the entirety of the OT as a web of symbols that must be understood as figural signifiers for Jesus and the life that he offers. In John's narrative, the Temple becomes a figural sign for Jesus' body. Likewise, the great feasts of Israel's worship are newly seen, in retrospect, to be replete with signs and symbols of Jesus: the pouring of water, the kindling of light, the rededication of the Temple, the good shepherd who truly feeds and heals God's people, and the Passover lamb. And even the scriptural narrative of Israel's redemption in the exodus becomes also a vast figural matrix, a story in which the manna from heaven signifies Jesus' flesh. All this works hermeneutically because, at the beginning and the end of the day, Jesus is the *Logos*, the Word present before creation. All creation breathes with *his* life. He is the divine Wisdom whose very being is the blueprint of all reality. So, for John, reading Scripture figurally—reading backwards in light of the story of Jesus—is a way of discerning the anticipatory traces of God the Word in his self-revelation to the world.

6

Retrospective Reading
The Challenges of Gospel-Shaped Hermeneutics

The Evangelists as Retrospective Scriptural Interpreters

We began this series of lectures by reflecting on Jesus' words in John 5: "If you believed Moses, you would believe me, for he wrote about me" (John 5:46). What could John the Evangelist mean by advancing such an audacious claim? In what sense can Moses be said to have written about Jesus? And what would it mean for us to believe that such an assertion might be true? What sort of hermeneutical landscape might open before us if we learned to read Israel's Scripture not only through the filtering lenses of modern critical methods but also through the eyes of John and the other authors of the canonical Gospels?[1]

The overall plan of these lectures has been simple: in the first lecture, I proposed the twofold thesis that the OT teaches us how to read the Gospels and that—at the same time—the Gospels teach us how to read the OT. The hermeneutical key to this intertextual dialectic is the practice of *figural reading*: the discernment of unexpected patterns of correspondence between earlier and later events or persons within a continuous temporal stream. In figural interpretation, the intertextual semantic effects can flow both directions: an earlier text can illuminate a later one, and vice versa. But the temporally ordered sequence of the two poles of a figural correspondence requires that the *comprehension* of the figure—the act of understanding that Erich Auerbach described as the *intellectus spiritualis*—must be retrospective.[2] Specifically with regard to the theme of these lectures, a figural christological reading of the OT is possible only retrospectively in light of Jesus' life, death, and resurrection. Thus, from the perspective of figural interpretation, it would be a hermeneutical blunder to read the Law and the Prophets as deliberately *predicting* events in the life of Jesus. But in light of the unfolding story of Jesus, it is both right and illuminating to *read backwards* and to discover in the Law and the Prophets an unexpected *foreshadowing* of the later story.

In the subsequent lectures, we have considered how each of the four Gospel writers performs the practice of reading backwards. We have sought to listen to the distinctive *voice* of each Evangelist and to delineate the ways in which each one draws upon Scripture—both explicitly and implicitly—in retelling the story of Jesus. I have suggested along the way that each one offers distinctive contributions, as well as distinctive challenges, for theological hermeneutics.

Our task in this final lecture, then, is to undertake some comparison and assessment. What are the strengths and weaknesses of the different hermeneutical approaches represented by the four Evangelists? Are there tensions among them? What do they share in common? Can or should we read the texts in the same ways they did? In particular, can we share their conviction that a retrospective reading of Israel's Scripture will disclose a mysterious Christology of divine identity? Should we concur with Udo Schnelle that "the OT is silent about Jesus Christ"? Or have we seen sufficient evidence to compel us to follow Martin Luther in seeing the OT as the swaddling cloths in which the Christ child is to be found by those who seek him? And, if Rowan Williams is right to describe the NT writings as the earliest stage in a "centuries-long task" of the "reorganization of Israel's religious language," should we regard that task as now finished? Or should we expect that we will continue to participate in the hermeneutical task that the Gospel writers began?

These are, of course, massive questions. As I ponder how they might be addressed in a single lecture, I would say something similar to what the puzzled Apostle Paul wrote to the Corinthians on the topic of virgins: "Now concerning virgins, I have no command of the Lord, but I give you my opinion as one who by the Lord's mercy is trustworthy" (1 Cor 7:25). I hope you will take the opinions I offer in this concluding lecture neither as a word from the Lord nor as definitive solutions to the problems posed in these lectures, but as a set of putatively trustworthy musings designed to invite you into a *conversation*—a conversation about matters that are of urgent interest for all who are concerned about the integrity and the future of Christian biblical interpretation.

So, let us first undertake a quick review of our findings in the previous lectures.

The multivocality of the Gospels. The Gospels offer us four distinctive voices; they do not speak in unison as interpreters of the OT. Rather, we should hear their testimonies as four distinctive voices singing in *polyphony.* If that is correct, the art of reading the Gospels is like the art of listening to choral singing. Each section in a choir must learn to hear and sing its own part. The choir director does not want everyone gravitating to sing the melody in unison; if that happens, the polyphony and the harmonic texture will be lost. So it is with the fourfold Gospel witness of the NT canon. To be sure, in a complex choral work, there may be moments of dissonance between the different parts. Discerning hearers do not want to eliminate the dissonances; rather, the task of appreciation is to develop a nuanced ability to hear how the dissonances belong to a larger artistic design.

At Duke Divinity School, we were privileged recently to host the U.S. premiere of a new *Saint Luke Passion* by the contemporary Scottish composer James MacMillan. In his notes for the program, Professor Jeremy Begbie wrote as follows:

> It is not surprising to find music of extremes in the *St. Luke Passion*— above all, a concentrated interplay between consonance and dissonance. Western music relies heavily on the engagement with, and resolution of, dissonance, and MacMillan draws on a huge variety of its techniques to evoke the redemption of discord which lies at the core of the passion narrative.[3]

The "concentrated interplay between consonance and dissonance" that Begbie describes is to be found not only in the passion narratives themselves and in MacMillan's musical rendering of them but also in the wider literary and theological design of the fourfold Gospel accounts. With that metaphor in mind, then, let us briefly review each of the four parts, each of the four Gospel witnesses, and ask whether they finally cohere in their polyphonic evocations of Israel's Scriptures.

Mark: Figuring the mystery of the kingdom. Mark delights in veiled, indirect allusion. For him the message of Israel's Scripture is an awesome μυστήριον that comes to its climactic, yet paradoxical, embodiment in the

figure of Jesus. Mark reads Scripture in a way that is relentlessly christological, while also insisting that recognition of Jesus' identity cannot be separated from costly discipleship that leads the disciple to take up the cross
and follow in the pattern defined by Jesus' death. Those who have ears to
hear and eyes to see will recognize that, in Jesus, God's power has broken
into the world and Isaiah's promised new exodus is being enacted—yet
in a way that thoroughly confounds human expectations. Mark shows
relatively little interest in Scripture as a repository of explicit predictions
about the Messiah; rather, for Mark, Scripture provides a rich symbolic
vocabulary that enables the Evangelist to adumbrate the astounding truth
about Jesus' divine identity. The man Jesus is somehow—in a way that
defies understanding—the God of Israel, present among us as the One
whom wind and sea obey, and yet at last nailed to a cross. The community of those to whom this apocalyptic secret is given may dare to speak
of this awful mystery only in hints, whispers, and scriptural allusions.
They are a community living in awe and anticipation, charged to wait and
to watch for that which has been hidden to be disclosed (Mark 4:21-25;
13:37). They are the possessors of a secret whose full revelation lies in
the future. Mark's hermeneutical strategy, therefore, is to provide cryptic
scriptural pointers that draw the discerning reader into the heart of the
eschatological mystery. This mysterious aspect of Mark's witness is aptly
characterized by the Greek Orthodox tradition, whose Vesperal Hymn
for the Feast of Mark the Evangelist acclaims him as "the herald of the
mystagogy of heaven" (τῆς οὐρανίου μυσταγωγίας τὸν κήρυκα).

What might we say, then, about the strengths and weaknesses of Mark's
distinctive strategy for engaging the OT in telling the story of Jesus?

The great strength of Markan hermeneutics lies in its distinctive
fusion of restraint and evocative power. Mark shows a reverent deference
to the hiddenness of divine mystery and the paradoxical character of revelation. It is precisely this deference that allows him fully to acknowledge the reality of suffering, the difficulty of discipleship, and the *not yet*
pole of eschatology. Mark's Jesus, precisely as the embodiment of Israel's
God, fully enters the realm of human suffering and models the costliness
of faithfulness in the present age. Mark's sober eschatological reserva-
tion also produces a healthy sense of the limits of human language and
a strong preference for communicating truth indirectly, through veiled
parabolic gesture.

What might be the weaknesses or drawbacks of Mark's artful account of the identity of Jesus? Most importantly, Mark's subtle indirection may allow many readers to miss the message of Jesus' divine identity— as indeed many NT critics in the modern era have done. Alongside the danger that veiled communication may leave many in the position of uncomprehending outsiders (Mark 4:10-12), Mark's hermeneutic is also susceptible to the characteristic pitfall of apocalyptic communities: the temptation to an excessive satisfaction in the possession of "insider" knowledge. Mark's full narrative constantly subverts the latter by show- ing how those to whom it should be given to know the μυστήριον con- stantly fail and misunderstand, while it is "outsiders" who respond rightly to Jesus. But in following Mark's hermeneutical strategy of allusive indi- rection, vigilance is necessary for us to avoid falling into the trap of smug aesthetic/epistemological superiority.[4]

Matthew: Torah transfigured. Matthew, on the other hand, is con- cerned to demonstrate as explicitly as possible how Jesus' life constituted the fulfillment of the OT. This fulfillment embraces both the coming-true of prophetic utterances (as in the formula quotations) and the narrative enactment of figural correspondences between Jesus and Israel. The latter deserves more attention than it has often been given in the interpretation of Matthew's Gospel; even the formula quotations are often richly allu- sive, depending for their full force on the device of metalepsis. They are meant to lead the reader back to recover their original context. Matthew seeks to show how Jesus reconfigures both Israel and Torah by carrying forward Israel's story—a story sketched in the genealogy as running from Abraham to David, from David to the Babylonian exile, and from the exile to the coming of Messiah Jesus (1:17). Jesus brings about the end of Israel's exile (depicted metaphorically in the birth and infancy narrative material as a return from Egypt) and creates a new community of disciples who are obedient from the heart to the true intention of the Torah—now disclosed by the sovereign divine authority of Jesus' teaching. Matthew's hermeneutical strategy, therefore, is to elucidate clearly how Jesus inter- prets and exemplifies Torah—a Torah now reconfigured around Jesus.

At the same time, however, for Matthew, Jesus is more than a messiah and lawgiver. The portrayal of Jesus as the enthroned Son of Man fig- ure who holds authority over heaven and earth (Daniel 7) is particularly crucial in Matthew for authorizing Israel's new mission to the nations and the revisionary hermeneutic that justifies it. Matthew's Son of Man Christology places the risen Jesus in the heavenly throne room, with power and authority that extends throughout all time and space.

Finally, at the heart of Matthew's account of the identity of Jesus lies the proclamation that Jesus is Emmanuel, the embodiment of the personal presence of Israel's God; he promises to be present with the gathered community of disciples until the end of the age. Accordingly, he rightly receives the worship of his followers, for he is the locus of God's presence in their midst.

What are the strengths and weaknesses of Matthew's hermeneutic? In some ways, they are the flip side of Mark's. In sharp contrast to Mark, Matthew offers his readers great clarity about how to approach the reading of Scripture and makes his operative hermeneutical filters explicit on the surface of the text. He draws clear lines of continuity with the story of Israel and overtly portrays Jesus as "God with us," the living presence of God who is to be worshiped as the holder of all authority. At the same time, Matthew also portrays Jesus as a teacher who both lays down guidelines for community life and frames a forceful scriptural apologetic for the Gentile mission as the logical extension and fulfillment of Israel's story. Thus, Matthew's robust Christology of divine identity lays the groundwork for a deep confidence in God's continuing guidance and presence in the church's life.

Are there drawbacks to Matthew's narrative portrayal of Jesus' identity? Three concerns might be mentioned. First, Matthew's strongly assertive christological position can sometimes bleed over into a harsh polemical stance toward other Jewish groups who represent different paradigms for interpreting Torah, as seen in the invective aimed at the scribes and Pharisees in Matthew 23. Second, while Matthew draws together many different biblical motifs, and while he projects the fulfillment of all of them onto the person of Jesus, it is not always clear that he has reflected systematically or coherently on how to integrate the resulting picture. How is it possible for Jesus to be simultaneously the figural fulfillment of Israel returning from exile, the new Moses who expounds Torah, and the actual embodiment of Israel's God eternally present to his people? It is not clear that Matthew has thought this through. Finally, in some cases, Matthew's fondness for overt confessional statement stands in some tension with Mark's reverent reticence before the divine mystery.

Does Matthew sometimes come close to recapitulating the enthusiastic error of Peter on the mountain of transfiguration (Matt 17:1-8): wanting to construct a fixed dwelling for Jesus, together with the Law and the Prophets, rather than simply listening and responding in awe and wonder?

Luke: The story of Israel's redemption. Luke, in contrast to Matthew's prediction-fulfillment schema, emphasizes *promise* and fulfillment. Israel's Scriptures are read by Luke principally as a treasury of God's promises to the covenant people. The fulfillment of these promises in Jesus is a demonstration of the faithfulness of Israel's God, a testimony that God has not forgotten "the promise he made to our ancestors, to Abraham and to his descendants forever" (Luke 1:55). Therefore, because Israel has languished in oppression, the fulfillment of Scripture entails "good news to the poor," "release to the captives" (Luke 4:18, citing Isa 61:1), and the doom of the rich and powerful. For Luke, the hallmark of right response to the message of Scripture is not so much obedience as *joy*: a glad and grateful reception of the powerful work of salvation performed by God throughout Israel's story; in the events of Jesus' life, death, and resurrection; and in the Spirit's continuing work in the church. Note that I just said, "performed *by God.*" Our study of Luke observed that Luke subtly identifies Jesus as the *Kyrios*, the one who is "Lord of all," the one who fulfills Isaiah's expectation of God as the Redeemer of Israel. His narrative thereby creates in the character of Jesus a paradoxical *Verbindungsidentität* that produces a much richer Christology of divine identity than modern NT criticism has tended to perceive.

Luke strongly highlights the continuity of the biblical story and its continuation in the *ekklesia*. The Spirit is "turning the world upside down" through the church (Acts 17:6) in such a way that the message of the kingdom of God presents a clear and radically *peaceful* alternative to the claims of the empire. But the good news for Israel also entails the corollary that those who do not recognize the time of their visitation by the *Kyrios*—those who refuse to listen to Jesus, the prophet like Moses—will be cut off from the people of God (Acts 3:22-23, citing Deut 18:15-20, Lev 23:29; cf. Luke 2:34-35). Luke's hermeneutical strategy, then, is to renarrate the story of Israel in such a way that the story of Jesus and the church can be confidently recognized as the fulfillment of the divine plan for salvation. That renarration typically involves not assertions about typological equivalences between Jesus and OT precursors but subtle echoing of OT motifs and narrative patterns, creating a "scriptural" symbolic world for the story of Jesus.

The strengths of Luke's hermeneutical strategy are very considerable. He boldly narrates the historical continuity between Israel's past, present, and future. His vision allows for a comprehensive appropriation of the things about Jesus "in all the scriptures": "the Law of Moses, the prophets, and the psalms" (24:44). He shows Jesus to be precisely the Lord of Israel who passionately seeks the redemption of the poor and downtrodden. And he also shows how the mission to the Gentiles is the outworking of God's longstanding plan for Israel as a light to the nations. His use of Scripture is characterized by allusive richness and, at the same time, a supple openness that lends itself well to apologetic engagement with outsiders and reasoned debate about the meanings of Israel's Scripture.

Weaknesses in Luke's hermeneutic? Many twentieth-century German critics suggested that Luke manifests an excessive confidence about the continuity of *Heilsgeschichte*, a potentially triumphalist reading of a smooth linearity that fails to reckon adequately with the disjunctive apocalyptic impact of the cross. I think this is a misguided criticism, an unsympathetic reading of Luke. Nonetheless, readers must take care not to fall into this trap. And this is of course one reason why we need Mark alongside Luke in the canon, as a counterweight to any possible triumphalism. In another respect, though, Luke and Mark stand closely together: both narrate the divine identity of Jesus in a way that depends more on subtle intertextual allusion than on the overt confessional claims favored by Matthew and John.

John: Refiguration of Israel's Temple and worship. As we noted in the last lecture, John focuses on fewer scriptural texts than the synoptic authors but develops them in a more artistically rounded way. He frames each scriptural image that he employs with luminous clarity against a dark background, like the figures at the center of Rembrandt's portraits. For John, the Psalms seem to play a dominant role in disclosing the identity of Jesus, while the Pentateuch—despite John's insistence that Moses wrote about Jesus—is not cited frequently. Strikingly, John tells his readers explicitly that Scripture can be understood only retrospectively after the resurrection; they are instructed to "read backwards" in light of the illumination provided by the Spirit who will come after Jesus' departure. And that retrospective reading will be explicitly *figural* in character.

John reads the entirety of the OT as a vast web of symbols that are to be read as figural signifiers for Jesus and the life that he offers. The Temple is a proleptic sign for Jesus' body. Israel's cultic practices and the great feasts of Israel's liturgical calendar are replete with signs and symbols of Jesus: the pouring of water and kindling of lights at the Feast of Tabernacles (Sukkoth); the rededication of the Temple by the good shepherd who truly feeds and heals God's people; the Passover Lamb whose bones are not broken; the bread that comes down from heaven to Israel in the wilderness. All these events and symbols point insistently to Jesus, who embodies that which they signified. When we read the story of Moses lifting up the serpent on a staff in the wilderness, we are to understand that we are reading a prefiguration of the lifting up of the Son of Man on the cross. The words of Moses are to be understood, then, in postresurrectional retrospect as figural foreshadowings of Jesus.

All this is possible for one compelling theological reason: Jesus is the incarnation of the *Logos* who was present before creation, through whom all things were made. All creation breathes with his life. He is the divine Wisdom whose very being is the blueprint of all reality. That is why he can declare, "I and the Father are one," both evoking and transforming Israel's *Shema*. So, for John, reading Scripture in this figural/symbolic fashion is nothing other than a way of discerning the pre-incarnational traces of the Word in his self-revelation to the world.

What are the strengths of John's highly distinctive way of reading Scripture? John offers us a profoundly *poetic* reading of the texts, and he is completely straightforward about setting forth his program of retrospective figural interpretation. This sweeping hermeneutical strategy enables a comprehensive reappropriation of Israel's sacred texts—and logically of everything else as well!—as metaphorically transparent to the Word that underlies and sustains all creation. This strategy may also have profound *apologetic* force in the historical aftermath of the crisis caused for Israel's worship life by the destruction of the Temple; the figural reading allows the spiritual reality that the Temple had signified to be absorbed into the body of Jesus, who now can offer life and wholeness to the whole world.

What about weaknesses? In the case of John, it might be better to speak not of "weaknesses" but of potential *dangers* in his hermeneutical strategy for reading the OT. It appears that his hermeneutic is framed polemically against rival interpreters; those who reject John's readings are characterized in the text as diabolical and ontologically estranged from God (John 8:39-47). This Gospel's approach to OT interpretation lends itself, therefore, all too readily to anti-Jewish and/or high-handedly supersessionist theologies. The text's apparent dualism can also open the door to forms of ahistorical quasi-gnostic spirituality. (It is for that reason that Irenaeus had to contend vigorously for an orthodox, early Catholic interpretation of John against Valentinian gnostics who found it congenial for their own theological purposes.)[5] I have suggested that John should be read neither as flatly supersessionist nor as hostile to continuity with Israel—but making that case fully convincing would take more time than I have. I will for now say only that the dualistic/gnostic interpretation of John makes the mistake of denying or denigrating the literal sense of Israel's Scriptures—whereas the *figural* reading that John practices does not deny the literal sense but completes it by linking it typologically with the narrative of Jesus and disclosing a deeper prefigurative truth within the literal historical sense.

The challenges of diversity. While these four different hermeneutical strategies might be in important respects complementary—indeed, their inclusion together in the NT canon represents the Christian tradition's judgment that they are so to be understood[6]—they represent distinctly different styles and sensibilities. It is difficult to imagine how any one community of faith could simultaneously embody all four approaches to Scripture with equal emphasis. One function of the church's canon, a diverse collection of writings, is to model a *repertoire* of faithful ways to receive and proclaim God's word. Particular voices within that canon will be more or less useful in different times and places, as the church discerns the points of vital intersection between the Bible and its immediate cultural situation. And perhaps one consequence of the canonization of such diverse texts is the de facto canonization of a principle of diversity: the very variety within the fourfold Gospel canon creates a stimulus and encouragement for us to carry on the story in our own voices, working out our own fresh ways of engaging Israel's Scripture. At the very least, inevitably, some choices have to be made about where the lines of emphasis will finally lie in our own appropriation of the scriptural witness.

For my own part, if I must declare my own sympathies with respect to the canonical Gospel writers as readers of Scripture, I find John the most problematical and Mark the most theologically generative in a postmodern era where direct speech about God is not a simple matter. And—candidly—I'm still trying to puzzle out what I think about Matthew.[7] A good argument can be made, however, that if we had to choose just one of the Gospels as a hermeneutical guide for the long haul, *Luke* offers the most adequate load-bearing narrative framework for the church's reading and proclamation of Scripture.

But given the diversity we have discerned, I want to ask another question: Is it possible still to hear our four witnesses as a polyphonic chorus singing different parts but in some sort of complex unity? Or—to shift away from a musical metaphor that may have carried about as much weight as it should—what would a fourfold Gospel-shaped hermeneutic look like? Do the Gospel writers, as interpreters of Scripture, converge and complement each other? What can we learn from reading them together and asking how their *common* fourfold witness might teach us to become better and more faithful readers? To that task I now turn in the final part of this lecture.

Gospel-Shaped Hermeneutics?

What would it mean to undertake the task of reading Scripture *along with* the Evangelists? First of all, it would mean cultivating a deep knowledge of the OT texts, getting these texts into our blood and bones. It would mean learning the texts by heart (in the fullest sense.) The pervasive, complex, and multivalent uses of Scripture that we find in the Gospels could arise only in and for a community immersed in scriptural language and imagery. Scripture provided the "encyclopedia of production" for the Evangelists' narration of the story of Jesus. Their way of pursuing what we call "doing theology" was to produce richly intertextual narrative accounts of the significance of Jesus. Because the language of the Bible was the Evangelists' native medium of expression, their reflection about God was articulated through subtle appropriations and adaptations of that linguistic medium. (For an analogy from a more recent time, consider the hymns of Charles Wesley: many of them are patchwork quilts of scriptural references and allusions.)[8]

How might *we* learn that language? We might do it partly through immersing ourselves in worship, since these texts are constitutive for the church's liturgical traditions; however, for those who are latecomers to those traditions, hard and intentional work may also be required. The American playwright Arthur Miller described his own arduous efforts to master the language of Shakespeare:

> You know what I used to do years ago? I would take any of Shakespeare's plays and simply copy them—pretending that I was him, you see. You know, it's a marvelous exercise. Just copy the speeches, and you gradually realize the concision, the packing together of experience, which is hard to do with just your ear. But if you have to work it with a pen or a piece of paper and you see that stuff coming together in the intense inner connection of sound and meaning, it's exhausting, just the thought of it.[9]

Miller's purpose in undertaking this "exhausting" exercise was of course not merely to transcribe Shakespeare's plays but to gain a grasp of the language that would enable him to move on and write his own. Our efforts to learn the Bible, similarly, have as their goal to empower us to speak God's word by renarrating the story of Jesus in our own speaking and writing.

It is precisely at that point that we stand to learn much from the four Evangelists. They provide for us paradigmatic models of how to receive and retell the scriptural story. In light of our study of their hermeneutical strategies, I would suggest at least ten ways that they might teach us how to read Scripture.

1. A Gospel-shaped hermeneutic necessarily entails *reading backwards*, reinterpreting Israel's Scripture in light of the story of Jesus. Such a reading is necessarily a *figural reading*, a reading that grasps patterns of correspondence between temporally distinct events, so that these events freshly illuminate each other. This means that for the Evangelists the "meaning" of the OT texts was not confined to the human author's original historical setting or to the meaning that could have been grasped by the original readers. Rather, Scripture was a complex body of texts given to the community by God, who had scripted the whole biblical drama in such a way that it had multiple senses.[10] Some of these senses are hidden, so that they come into focus only *retrospectively*.

2. More specifically, Scripture is to be reinterpreted in light of the cross and resurrection. There is no reason to be embarrassed about this, because the Evangelists were convinced that the events of Jesus' life and death and resurrection were in fact *revelatory*: they disclosed the key to understanding all that had gone before. Of course, this involves reassessment and

transformation. After the resurrection, the community of Jesus' followers returns to reread Scripture under the guidance of the Spirit and experiences, again and again, an "Aha!" reaction. Their eyes are opened anew to see how Moses and prophets *prefigure* Jesus. The Gospel of John offers the most explicit account of this hermeneutical reality in its interpretation of Jesus' words about raising up the destroyed Temple: "After he was raised from the dead, his disciples remembered that he had said this; and they believed the scripture and the word that Jesus had spoken" (John 2:22). Luke paints a similar picture in his resurrection appearance narratives, where it is only the Risen Lord who opens the minds of the disciples to understand Scripture. And even Mark, that most restrained of narrators, shows us that it is only after the death of Jesus that any human character—in this case the Roman centurion—first perceives his true identity as Son of God (Mark 15:39).

3. Similarly, the Evangelists' diverse imaginative uses and transformations of the OT texts summon us also to a *conversion of the imagination.* We can hear their proclamation only if we allow their intertextual performances to retrain our sensibilities as readers. And—here is a point I have been making repeatedly in these lectures—if we learn from them how to read, we will approach the reading of Scripture with a heightened awareness of *story, metaphor, prefiguration, allusion, echo, reversal, and irony.* To read Scripture well, we must bid farewell to plodding literalism and rationalism in order to embrace *a complex poetic sensibility.* The Gospel writers are trying to teach us to become more interesting people—by teaching us to be more interesting readers.

4. For the Evangelists, Israel's Scripture told the true *story* of the world. Scripture was not merely a repository of ancient writings containing important laws or ideas or images; rather, it traced out a coherent story line that stretched from creation, through the election of Israel, to the *telos* of God's redemption of the world.[11] (This point emerges with particular force in Luke's account, but Mark and Matthew share a similar vision. Even John presupposes this narrative framework, as shown by his references to Abraham, Jacob, Moses, Israel's Passover and wilderness traditions, Isaiah, and so forth.) One significant implication of this is that a Gospel-shaped hermeneutic will pay primary attention to large narrative arcs and patterns in the OT, rather than treating Scripture chiefly as a source of oracles, prooftexts, or halakhic regulations. The Evangelists,

who are themselves storytellers, are much more interested in the OT as story than as prediction or as law.

5. It is important to emphasize that the Evangelists' retrospective reinterpretation of Israel's story is in no sense a negation or rejection of that story. It is, rather, the story's transfiguration and continuation. This is one of the features that marks the distinction between the canonical Gospels and those later extracanonical writings that either ignore or repudiate Israel and Israel's God. The canonical Evangelists understand themselves to be standing *within* the still-unfolding narrative trajectory of Israel's covenantal relationship with the God of Abraham, Isaac, and Jacob. This means not only that their narratives emphatically exclude the later Marcionite mutation of Christian theology but also that their account of the identity of Jesus must be understood within the framework of Israel's fierce loyalty to the one God of all the earth—a point to which we shall return in a few moments.

6. The Gospel writers approach Scripture as a unified whole, but their reading of it is not undifferentiated. Each of the Evangelists seems to operate with a de facto canon within the canon, giving more attention to some parts of Scripture than to others. At one level, this involves a particularly intense focus on certain books: above all the Pentateuch, Isaiah, and the Psalms. Each Gospel writer varies the "mix" of attention given to the different OT witnesses, rather like a recording engineer adjusting the volume of different tracks in the recording studio; for example, Matthew turns up the volume on the prophets, and John puts the Psalms at the forefront of his mix. In some cases, it appears that this sort of intracanonical focus is given not to whole OT books but to particular selected passages, such as Isaiah 40 (the announcement of the end of Israel's exile) or Daniel 7:13-14 (the account of the glorified, enthroned Son of Man). Such passages provide privileged "viewpoints" from which to survey the whole of Scripture.

7. With regard to the question of canon, it is probably worth mentioning something I have been assuming throughout these lectures, though not directly arguing: the Scripture employed by the Evangelists is, on the whole, the Greek Bible (LXX). With all due allowances made for particular cases in which an OT citation may seem to reflect a Hebrew textual tradition over against the text known to us in the Greek versions (for instance, Matt 2:15: "Out of Egypt have I called my son"), it appears that

the functional Bible for the communities in and for which the Gospels were composed was a Greek translation. This has potentially interesting implications for how we think about what we mean when we speak about the Christian Bible. Should we conclude that Augustine, who preferred the LXX, had the better of the argument against Jerome, who wanted to privilege the Hebrew text? Scholars such as Luke Timothy Johnson and David Moessner have been advocating a recovery of the Septuagint as the primary Christian Old Testament.[12] In light of the Evangelists' actual citation practices, the proposal is worth considering.

8. Because the Evangelists are so deeply immersed in Israel's Scripture, their references and allusions to it are characteristically *metaleptic* in character: that is, they nudge the discerning reader to recognize and recover the context from which the intertextual references are drawn. In many, many instances, a consideration of the fuller original context will shed light on the story the Evangelists are telling and add important nuance to an otherwise flat surface reading. To illustrate, let us recall a single example from an earlier lecture: when Luke concludes the story of Jesus' healing of a crippled, bent-over woman, he remarks that "all those who oppose him were put to shame" (Luke 13:17). When we hear in these words the explicit echo of Isa 45:16 LXX, Luke's simple narrative explodes with larger christological significance, for in Isaiah it is precisely the enemies of "the God of Israel, the Savior" who are put to shame. Such evocative hints make a serious demand on the reader-competence of the Gospel's audience, but they also offer serious hermeneutical rewards for those with ears to hear.

9. And now I come at last to the central substantive thesis that has emerged for me with increasing force the more I have tried to work my way into learning from the Evangelists how to read Scripture. *The more deeply we probe the Jewish and OT roots of the Gospel narratives, the more clearly we see that each of the four Evangelists, in their diverse portrayals, identifies Jesus as the embodiment of the God of Israel.* This finding runs against the grain of much NT scholarship, which has supposed that the earliest and most "Jewish" Christology is a "low" Christology, in which Jesus is a prophet, teacher of wisdom, and proclaimer of the coming kingdom of God, but not a divine figure. The judgment of Bart Ehrman in a recent book expresses this typical position: "The idea that Jesus was divine was a later Christian invention, one found, among our gospels, only in John."[13]

At least since the nineteenth century, it has been axiomatic among critical biblical scholars that the "high" Christology of John's Gospel is a late
Hellenistic development—and that the more one focuses on the synoptic
tradition and locates Jesus within a monotheistic Jewish/OT context, the
more improbable it would seem to identify him as divine.[14] What we have
seen in these lectures, however, is that it is precisely through drawing on
OT images that all four Gospels portray the identity of Jesus as mysteriously fused with the identity of God. This is true even of Mark and Luke,
the two Synoptic Gospels usually thought to have the "lowest" or most
"primitive" Christologies. This is not to deny that the Jesus of the Gospels
is a human figure. On the contrary, the very same Gospels that identify
him as Israel's God simultaneously portray him as a man who hungers,
suffers, and dies on a cross. Thereby, they create the stunning paradoxes
that the church's later dogmatic controversies sought to address in order
to formulate a theological grammar adequate to respect the narrative tensions inescapably posed by the Gospels. The Gospel narratives, precisely
through their reading of the OT to identify Jesus, force us to rethink
what we mean when we say the word "God."[15] This point has never been
more forcefully expressed than by Karl Barth in Part IV/1 of his *Church
Dogmatics*:

> We may believe that God can and must only be absolute in contrast to all
> that is relative, exalted in contrast to all that is lowly, active in contrast
> to all suffering, inviolable in contrast to all temptation, transcendent in
> contrast to all immanence, and therefore divine in contrast to everything
> human, in short that He can and must be only the "Wholly Other." But
> such beliefs are shown to be quite untenable, and corrupt and pagan, by
> the fact that God does in fact be and do this in Jesus Christ.[16]

To Barth's declaration, all four canonical Evangelists would say *Amen*: the
Gospels narrate the story of how the God of Israel was embodied in Jesus.
This means, *inter alia*, that we should stop using the terms "high" Chris-
tology and "low" Christology to characterize the four canonical Gospels.
These very categories presuppose an a priori philosophical account of
"God" that the Gospel narratives contradict.

10. Finally, the Evangelists consistently approach Scripture with the
presupposition that the God found in the stories of the OT is living and
active. It is for that reason—and only for that reason—that the hermeneutic I have been describing can be embraced as *truthful*. It is not an

exercise in literary fantasy like, say, trying to live inside the imaginative world of the *Lord of the Rings* trilogy or the *Star Wars* films. Rather, all of the hermeneutical recommendations I have enumerated here make sense only because God is the primary agent at work in and through the biblical story—and, indeed, only because God is in some ultimate sense the author of Israel's story. The one Lord confessed in Israel's *Shema* is the same God actively at work in the death and resurrection of Jesus Christ. Apart from the truth of that claim, any talk of the unity of the OT and the NT is simply nonsense. There is only one reason why christological interpretation of the OT is not a matter of stealing or twisting Israel's sacred texts: the God to whom the Gospels bear witness, the God incarnate in Jesus, is the same as the God of Abraham, Isaac, and Jacob. Either that is true, or it is not. If it is not, the Gospels are a delusional and pernicious distortion of Israel's story. If it is true, then the figural literary unity of Scripture, OT and NT together, is nothing other than the climactic fruition of that one God's self-revelation. As readers, we are forced to choose which of these hermeneutical forks in the road we will take.

I propose that if we *are* able to follow the Evangelists' guidance on how to read, we will gain crucial resources for renarrating the story of Jesus in an age when once again we must articulate the gospel in a fragmented world urgently seeking signs of hope. So, let the intertextual conversation continue. By seeing Israel's Scripture through the eyes of the Gospel writers, may we be encouraged to read backwards—and empowered to carry forward the story of Jesus with new freedom and faithfulness.

Notes

Preface

1 Richard B. Hays, *Echoes of Scripture in the Letters of Paul* (New Haven: Yale University Press, 1989).

2 In this way, the present study differs in its intent from the important work of Larry Hurtado, *Lord Jesus Christ: Devotion to Jesus in Earliest Christianity* (Grand Rapids: Eerdmans, 2003).

3 Markus Bockmuehl, email correspondence, June 13, 2014, emphasis in original. See also his book *Seeing the Word: Refocusing New Testament Study* (Grand Rapids: Baker Academic, 2006).

4 Hays, *Echoes*, 176–77.

5 On figural interpretation, see chap. 1, below.

6 Warren Buffett quoted in David Segal, "In Letter, Warren Buffett Concedes a Tough Year," *New York Times*, February 28, 2009, http://www.nytimes.com/2009/03/01/business/01buffett.html.

7 For an account of the rhetorical art of Obama's speech, see James Wood, "Victory Speech," *New Yorker*, November 17, 2008.

8 For a general discussion of intertextual interpretation, see my essay, "'Who Has Believed Our Message?' Paul's Reading of Isaiah," in *The Conversion of the Imagination: Paul as Interpreter of Israel's Scripture* (Grand Rapids: Eerdmans, 2005), 25–49. For a more technical introduction to the issues, see Stefan Alkier, "Intertextuality and the Semiotics of Biblical Texts," in *Reading the Bible Intertextually* (ed. Richard B. Hays, Stefan Alkier, and Leroy A. Huizenga; Waco, Tex.: Baylor University Press, 2009), 3–21.

9 For close textual study of the linguistic character of the scriptural texts used by the Matthew and John, see M. J. J. Menken, *Matthew's Bible: The Old Testament Text of the Evangelist* (BETL 173; Leuven: Peeters, 2004); idem, *Old Testament Quotations in the Fourth Gospel: Studies in Textual Form* (Kampen: Kok Pharos, 1996).

10 See Mark Goodacre, *The Case against Q: Studies in Markan Priority and the Synoptic Problem* (Harrisburg, Pa.: Trinity International, 2002).

11 C. H. Dodd, *According to the Scriptures: The Sub-structure of New Testament Theology* (London: Nisbet, 1952).

12 Barnabas Lindars, *New Testament Apologetic: The Doctrinal Significance of the Old Testament Quotations* (Philadelphia: Westminster, 1961).

13 A number of Dahl's important essays are conveniently gathered in Nils A. Dahl, *Jesus the Christ: The Historical Origins of Christian Doctrine* (ed. Donald Juel; Minneapolis: Fortress, 1991). For Juel's own contribution, see Donald Juel, *Messianic Exegesis: Christological Interpretation of the Old Testament in Early Christianity* (Philadelphia: Fortress, 1988).

14 Hans W. Frei, *The Eclipse of Biblical Narrative: A Study in Eighteenth and Nineteenth Century Hermeneutics* (New Haven: Yale University Press, 1974); idem, *The Identity of Jesus Christ: The Hermeneutical Bases of Dogmatic Theology* (Philadelphia: Fortress, 1975).

15 Joel Marcus, *The Way of the Lord: Christological Exegesis of the Old Testament in the Gospel of Mark* (Louisville, Ky.: Westminster John Knox, 1992). Idem, *Mark: A New Translation with Introduction and Commentary*, 2 vols. (AB 27 and 27A; New York: Doubleday, 2000–2009); the individual volume titles are *Mark 1–8* and *Mark 8–16*.

16 N. T. Wright, *Jesus and the Victory of God* (London: SPCK, 1996; Minneapolis: Fortress, 1996); idem, *How God Became King: The Forgotten Story of the Gospels* (New York: HarperOne, 2012).

17 Larry Hurtado, *One God, One Lord: Early Christian Devotion and Ancient Jewish Monotheism* (Edinburgh: T&T Clark, 1988); idem, *Lord Jesus Christ* (see n. 2 above). For an important precursor to Hurtado's work, see Martin Hengel, *Between Jesus and Paul: Studies in the Earliest History of Christianity* (Philadelphia: Fortress, 1983; repr., Waco, Tex.: Baylor University Press, 2013).

18 Richard Bauckham, *God Crucified: Monotheism and Christology in the New Testament* (Grand Rapids: Eerdmans, 1999); this concise work was subsequently incorporated into a larger collection of his essays, *Jesus and the God of Israel: God Crucified and Other Studies on the New Testament's Christology of Divine Identity* (Grand Rapids: Eerdmans, 2008).

19 Daniel Boyarin, *Border Lines: The Partition of Judaeo-Christianity* (Philadelphia: University of Pennsylvania Press, 2004).

20 C. Kavin Rowe, *Early Narrative Christology: The Lord in the Gospel of Luke* (BZNW 139; Berlin: de Gruyter, 2006; Grand Rapids: Baker Academic, 2009).

21 For the essays produced by this project, see Beverly R. Gaventa and Richard B. Hays, eds., *Seeking the Identity of Jesus: A Pilgrimage* (Grand Rapids: Eerdmans, 2008). The participants in this venture were Dale Allison, Gary Anderson, Markus Bockmuehl, Sarah Coakley, Brian Daley, Beverly Roberts Gaventa, A. Katherine Grieb, Richard Hays, Robert Jenson, Joel Marcus, Walter Moberly, William Placher, Katherine Sonderegger, David Steinmetz, Marianne Meye Thompson, and Francis Watson.

22 See Christopher B. Hays' programmatic essay, "Echoes of the Ancient Near East? Intertextuality and the Comparative Study of the Old Testament," in *The Word Leaps the Gap: Essays on Scripture and Theology in Honor of Richard B. Hays* (ed. J. Ross Wagner, C. Kavin Rowe, and A. Katherine Grieb; Grand Rapids: Eerdmans, 2008), 20–43. To see how this program is worked out more fully in practice, see Christopher B. Hays, *Death in the Iron Age II and in 1 Isaiah* (FAT 79; Tübingen: Mohr Siebeck, 2011).

Chapter 1

1   Martin Luther, "Preface to the Old Testament," in *Luther's Works*, vol. 35 (ed. E. Theodore Bachmann; Philadelphia: Muhlenberg, 1960), 235–36. I am indebted to Tucker Ferda for calling my attention to this passage.

2   Erich Auerbach, *Mimesis* (Princeton: Princeton University Press, 1968), 73. See also Auerbach's detailed essay, "Figura," in *Time, History, and Literature: Selected Essays of Erich Auerbach* (ed. James I. Porter, trans. Jane O. Newman; Princeton: Princeton University Press, 2014), 65–113.

3   For an account of these categories, see Alkier, "Intertextuality," in Hays, Alkier, and Huizenga, *Reading the Bible Intertextually*.

4   Frei, *Eclipse*, esp. 18–37 on figural interpretation in the Protestant Reformers.

5   Frei, *Eclipse*, 33.

6   Udo Schnelle, *Theology of the New Testament* (Grand Rapids: Baker, 2009), 52, emphasis in original. German original: "Eine Biblische Theologie is nicht möglich, weil 1) das Alte Testament von Jesus Christus *schweigt*, 2) die Auferstehung *eines Gekreuzigten* von den Toten als kontingentes Geschehen sich in keine antike Sinnbildung integrieren lässt." *Theologie des Neuen Testaments* (Göttingen: Vandenhoeck & Ruprecht, 2007), 40. Schnelle also gives a third reason for the impossibility of a biblical theology: "[W]hile the Old Testament can be thought of as the most important cultural and theological context for understanding the New Testament, it is by no means the only one" (52). It is unclear to me why this undeniably true observation should make it *impossible* to articulate a biblical theology.

7   See Richard B. Hays, "Reading Scripture in Light of the Resurrection," in *The Art of Reading Scripture* (ed. Ellen F. Davis and Richard B. Hays; Grand Rapids: Eerdmans, 2003), 216–38.

8   My hope, however, is that these lectures might encourage many students of Scripture to arrive at home and to know the place for the first time.

9   David Lodge, *Small World: An Academic Romance* (London: Secker & Warburg, 1984), 51–52.

10 For those who need the joke explained, the command to love God with all your heart and soul and strength, quoted by Jesus in Mark 12:29-30 and parallels, comes from Deut 6:5, and it is at the heart of daily prayer in the Jewish tradition.

11 Dietrich Bonhoeffer, *Widerstand und Ergebung: Briefe und Aufzeichnungen aus der Haft* (ed. Christian Gremmels, Eberhard Bethge, and Renata Bethge, in collaboration with Ilse Tödt; Gütersloh: Chr. Kaiser, 1998), 226. German original: "Wer zu schnell und zu direkt neutestamentlich sein und empfinden will, ist m. E. kein Christ." I am indebted to Ellen Davis for this reference.

12 I.e., Jesus is not merely seeking to reform current practices and gain minimal access for Gentiles to the outer court of the Temple; rather, his symbolic action points more radically to a future in which all nations enter the Temple alongside Israel to praise God. This eschatological scenario is rarely sufficiently recognized in commentaries on Mark. The best discussion is to be found in Rikk E. Watts, *Isaiah's New Exodus and Mark* (WUNT 2. Reihe 88; Tübingen: Mohr Siebeck, 1997), 318–25. My discussion of this example focuses on the Markan form of the story. Interestingly, both Matthew and Luke omit from the Isaiah quotation the words πᾶσιν τοῖς ἔθνεσιν ("for

all the nations"). This agreement against Mark interestingly problematizes the usual two-source hypothesis about synoptic relations. It would appear that both Matthew and Luke are concerned, in different ways, to reserve the emphasis on Gentile mission for the postresurrection period. For detailed discussion, see Mark Goodacre, "The Evangelists' Use of the Old Testament and the Synoptic Problem," in *New Studies in the Synoptic Problem: Oxford Conference, April 2008; Essays in Honour of Christopher M. Tuckett* (ed. P. Foster, A. Gregory, J. S. Kloppenborg, and J. Verheyden; BETL 239; Leuven: Peeters, 2011), 281–98.

13 E. P. Sanders, *Jesus and Judaism* (Philadelphia: Fortress, 1985), 61–76; quotation from p. 75.

14 "New Testament scholars who write about Jesus' concern for the purity of the temple seem to have in mind a familiar Protestant idea: 'pure' worship consists in the Word, and all external rites should be purged. . . . I think that we should drop the discussion of Jesus' action as one concerned with purifying the worship of God." Sanders, *Jesus and Judaism*, 67–68.

15 Sanders regards Jesus' prophecy of the Temple's destruction chiefly as a prelude to the vision of its eschatological restoration, rather than as a judgment on Israel's unfaithfulness or as a call for national repentance. This would explain in part why Sanders resists seeing the Jeremiah citation as an authentic saying of Jesus. I am indebted to Richard Bauckham for emphasizing this point in correspondence following my presentation of this lecture in Cambridge.

16 For an elegant exposition of this reading of Mark 11:12-26, see Morna D. Hooker, *The Gospel according to Saint Mark* (BNTC; London: A&C Black, 1991), 260–70. This interpretation of the story of the withered fig tree is challenged by Philip F. Esler, "The Incident of the Withered Fig Tree in Mark 11: A New Source and Redactional Explanation," *JSNT* 28 (2005): 41–67. Esler's argument is remarkably dismissive of the power of intertextual allusion. (He writes: "If Mark wished to convey a message of judgment about to fall on Israel, why did he simply not have his Jesus refer to some of the Old Testament material Hooker cites, especially Jer 8.13[?]. If Hooker were correct, Mark would be an incompetent communicator.") One might well ask where the deficiency in competence lies: in Mark as communicator, or in Esler as reader?

17 Interestingly, the Gospel of Thomas retains a vestigial reduction of the imagery of Psalm 118: "Jesus said: Show me the stone which the builders rejected. It is the cornerstone" (GosT 66). The fact that this saying directly follows Thomas' version of the parable of the Wicked Tenants (GosT 65)—though without any narrative connection to the parable—is one significant piece of evidence that GosT is actually derivative from the synoptic tradition.

18 See, e.g., Robert W. Funk, Roy W. Hoover, et al., *The Five Gospels* (New York: Macmillan, 1993), 510–11.

19 On Thomas' general disregard for the OT, see Mark Goodacre, *Thomas and the Gospels: The Case for Thomas's Familiarity with the Synoptics* (Grand Rapids: Eerdmans, 2012), 187–91. Goodacre draws particular attention to Gospel of Thomas 52: "His disciples said to him, 'Twenty-four prophets spoke in Israel, and all of them spoke in you.' He said to them, 'You have omitted the one living in your presence and have

spoken [only] of the dead.'" Goodacre then comments, "There is a straightforward disdain here for the Scriptures. Jesus is the 'Living One'; the prophets of the Old Testament are 'the dead'" (188).

20 Interestingly, Luke's editing of the Markan material already eliminates some of the details from Isaiah 5 and abbreviates the citation of Psalm 118. On the other hand, Luke agrees with Matthew in adding an allusion to Dan 2:34-35, 44-45 (Matt 21:44 / Luke 20:18).

21 As Anna Maria Schwermer has suggested, one way of reading their blindness is to see it as Luke's narrative figuration of the larger problem of Israel's failure to comprehend the salvation offered in Jesus. The story parallels Paul's account of the "veil" that occludes Israel's understanding of Scripture: "[T]heir minds were hardened. Indeed, to this very day, when they hear the reading of the old covenant, that same veil is still there, since only in Christ is it set aside. Indeed, to this very day whenever Moses is read, a veil lies over their minds" (2 Cor 3:14-15). Anna Maria Schwermer, "Der Auferstandene und die Emmausjünger," in *Auferstehung—Resurrection* (ed. Friedrich Avemarie and Hermann Lichtenberger; Tübingen: Mohr Siebeck, 2001), 95–117.

22 I am persuaded by C. F. Evans' suggestion that the rebuke should be translated, "Oh, how foolish you are, and how slow of heart to become believers *on the basis of* all that the prophets had said." C. F. Evans, *Saint Luke* (TPINTC; London: SCM Press, 1990), 910.

23 R. W. L. Moberly, *The Bible, Theology, and Faith: A Study of Abraham and Jesus* (Cambridge Studies in Christian Doctrine; Cambridge: Cambridge University Press, 2000), 51.

24 Moberly, *Bible, Theology, and Faith*, 51.

25 Moberly (*Bible, Theology, and Faith*, 51–52) points out that Luke's portrayal of Jesus' identity throughout his Gospel draws on Old Testament texts—e.g., the Spirit-anointed Servant of Isa 61 in Luke 4:16-21. The point is well taken, but most of the examples offered by Moberly do not clearly demonstrate the pattern of suffering and glorification of which Luke 24:26 speaks. The pattern appears more unambiguously in the Acts material (e.g., Acts 2:22-36; 4:24-30; 13:26-41).

26 Moberly states the point concisely: "Christian understanding is inseparable from a certain kind of 'eucharistic' lifestyle and practice. It is to those who are willing to live and act as Jesus did that the way Jesus understood God and scripture is most likely to make sense." Moberly, *Bible, Theology, and Faith*, 66. Moberly intends the term "eucharistic" to refer not just to liturgical ceremonies but to a broad range of practices that are "symbolically suggestive of the kind of action through which Jesus, the Christ, welcomed people and mediated God's kingdom to them" (65).

CHAPTER 2

1 "This took place to fulfill what had been spoken through the prophet, saying,
'Tell the daughter of Zion,
Look, your king is coming to you,
humble, and mounted on a donkey,
and on a colt, the foal of a donkey.'"

2   Alan F. Segal (*Two Powers in Heaven: Early Rabbinic Reports about Christianity and Gnosticism* [SJLA; Leiden: Brill, 1977; repr., Waco, Tex.: Baylor University Press, 2012]) has shown how the later rabbinic polemic against "two powers in heaven" was directed against various Jewish traditions that included, *inter alia*, the NT writers' application of apocalyptic passages such as Dan 7:13-14 to Jesus. Daniel Boyarin ("The Gospel of the *Memra*: Jewish Binitarianism and the Prologue to John," *HTR* 94 [2001]: 243–84) has contended provocatively that, despite the rabbinic effort to suppress this "heresy," some form of "binitarianism" was "the religious Koine of Jews in Palestine and the Diaspora" (260); see also Boyarin's subsequent elaboration of this thesis in *Border Lines*. For a study that places particular emphasis on exegesis of Daniel 7 as a key to NT Christology, see Boyarin, *The Jewish Gospels: The Story of the Jewish Christ* (New York: New Press, 2011). The traditions described by these studies provide a background against which Mark's narrative portrayal of Jesus can be plausibly understood.

3   On the question of "divine identity Christology" in the Gospels, see the paradigm-changing work of Richard Bauckham, *God Crucified*; this concise work was subsequently incorporated into a larger collection of his essays, *Jesus and the God of Israel*. Bauckham's provocative treatment of this topic has significantly influenced my thinking about the topics treated in these lectures. Also significant in this context is the earlier work of Larry Hurtado, *One God, One Lord*, subsequently developed on a larger canvas in his magnum opus, *Lord Jesus Christ*. Hurtado argues that "the binitarian devotion of early Christianity was an innovation initiated by Jewish Christians loyal to their ancestral concern for the uniqueness of God" (*One God, One Lord*, 124). He suggests that such devotional practices were a "mutation" of earlier Jewish beliefs about exalted intermediary "divine agent" figures. Bauckham, by contrast, contends that the gap between the Creator God and any created "agent" is too vast to be explained by Hurtado's hypothesis about the origins of belief in the divinity of Jesus.

4   Watts, *Isaiah's New Exodus*, 80.

5   Although *Kyrios* is not a common Markan epithet for Jesus (in contrast to Luke), several passages in Mark do connect this title to Jesus: Mark 2:28; 11:3; and 12:36-37. See Marcus, *Way of the Lord*, 38–39. To Marcus' list of passages, I would add 5:19.

6   Interestingly, the fifth-century uncial manuscript W continues the citation of Isaiah 40 to include the entirety of Isa 40:3-8. This certainly does not reflect the original text of Mark's Gospel, but it does show that some early readers of the text were acutely interested in the fuller Isaian framework of Mark's citation.

7   In his recent study, *The Preexistent Son* (pp. 249–52), Simon Gathercole cautiously advances the suggestion, following the lead of several German scholars, that the scriptural citation in Mark 1:2 ("See, I am sending my messenger ahead of *you*, who will prepare *your* way") should be interpreted as a heavenly court utterance, evoking an imagined "prehistoric scene" in which God the Father addresses the Son about the preparation for his impending mission of being sent into the world. We of course have ample analogies for this sort of reading of Scripture in the Letter to the Hebrews (e.g., Heb 1:5-14). Even within Mark's own narrative, there is one very clear example

in 12:35-37, in which we hear in the words of Ps 110:1, "the one Kyriòs speaking in heaven to the other." Gathercole, *The Preexistent Son: Recovering the Christologies of Matthew, Mark, and Luke* (Grand Rapids: Eerdmans, 2006), 251; citing Johannes Schreiber, *Die Markuspassion: Eine redaktionsgeschichtliche Untersuchung* (BZNW 68; Berlin: de Gruyter, 1993), 238. (Interestingly, Ps 110:1 also appears in Heb 1:13, explicitly interpreted as God's address to Jesus.) Gathercole, whose discussion focuses on the question of Jesus' *preexistence* rather than the question of his *divine identity*, is uncertain whether to accept this interpretation in relation to Mark 1:2-3. It seems to me, on the whole, the likeliest interpretation of the text, even though Mark, yet again, leaves significant ambiguity in his spare narration.

8   See Rudolf Bultmann, *History of the Synoptic Tradition* (New York: Harper & Row, 1963), 212–13.

9   J. Marcus (*Mark 1–8*, 222) rightly suggests that the phrasing of the question (τίς δύναται ἀφιέναι ἁμαρτίας εἰ μὴ εἷς ὁ θεός [literally, "Who is able to forgive sins except One, i.e., God"]) recalls the *Shema* (Deut 6:4). The same phrasing is echoed in Jesus' encounter with the rich inquirer (Mark 10:18): τί με λέγεις ἀγαθόν; οὐδεὶς ἀγαθὸς εἰ μὴ εἷς ὁ θεός ("Why do you call me good? No one is good except One, i.e., God"). The discerning reader will recognize that—in light of other evidence in the Gospel—the rich inquirer has spoken more truly than he realizes.

10 For other similar accounts of divine forgiveness of sins, see Isa 44:22; Ps 103:3; Ps 130:3-4.

11 Marcus, *Mark 1–8*, 222–23. Marcus also intriguingly suggests that the phrase "so that you may know" in Mark 2:10 echoes the wording of Moses' confrontational speeches to Pharaoh in Egypt (Exod 9:13b-14; cf. Exod 8:10, 22; 10:2).

12 "Thus, for Mark, the heavenly God remains the ultimate forgiver, but at the climax of history he has delegated his power of absolution to a 'Son of Man' who carries out his gracious will in the earthly sphere." Marcus, *Mark 1–8*, 223.

13 Psalm 107 is by no means the only OT passage that speaks of God's authority over wind and waves. Cf. Job 38:8-11; Ps 65:7; 89:9. For the image of God's rebuking the sea, see also Job 26:10-12; Ps 104:5-9; 106:8-12; Isa 51:9-11.

14 The expression "like sheep without a shepherd" was a proverbial way of describing Israel's plight after the demise of a king or under inept or wicked rulers (e.g., 1 Kgs 22:17; 2 Chr 18:16; Zech 10:2; Judith 11:19). This passage echoes both Num 27:17 and Ezekiel 34 and thereby hints that Jesus is to be the new messianic shepherd of the people who will "lead them out and bring them in" and provide protection and sustenance. He thus assumes a role typologically prefigured by Joshua (Ἰησοῦς) and David.

15 E.g., Hooker, *Gospel according to Saint Mark*, 169. Ps 77:19-20 would provide a particularly nice link to the feeding of the five thousand, since it speaks of God leading his people "like a flock."

16 The LXX's περιπατῶν . . . ἐπὶ θαλάσσης (Job 9:8) may be compared to Mark's ἐπὶ τῆς θαλάσσης περιπατοῦντα (Mark 6:49).

17 Augustine, *The Harmony of the Gospels* 2.47, as translated by Thomas C. Oden and Christopher A. Hall, eds., *Mark* (ACCS; Downers Grove, Ill.: InterVarsity, 1998), 95.

18 The Hebrew text of Job 9:11 reads: הֵן יַעֲבֹר עָלַי וְלֹא אֶרְאֶה וְיַחֲלֹף וְלֹא־אָבִין לוֹ. The last clause could well be translated as "and I do not understand him," a rendering that would make the citation even more telling as an intertextual counterpoint to Mark 6:45-52. The verb עבר ("pass by") is often translated in the LXX as παρελθεῖν (as in Exod 33:19, 22; and 34:6). The LXX translator of Job, however, has used παρελθεῖν in the second clause of 9:11 (to render חלף) rather than in the first.

19 Commentators regularly note the possibility of an allusion to Job 9:8 in Mark 6:45-52. Of the commentaries I have consulted, only William L. Lane (*The Gospel according to Mark* [NICNT; Grand Rapids: Eerdmans, 1974], 236) notes the possible significance of Job 9:11 for understanding Mark's reference to Jesus' intent to "pass by" the disciples.

20 Rudolf Pesch, *Das Markusevangelium* (HTKNT 2; Freiburg-Basel-Vienna: Herder, 1976), 1:361; J. P. Heil, *Jesus Walking on the Sea: Meaning and Gospel Functions of Matt 14:22-33, Mark 6:45-52, and John 6:15b-21* (Analecta Biblica 87; Rome: Pontifical Institute, 1981), 69–72; Marcus, *Mark 1–8*, 426. See also 1 Kgs 19:11-13.

21 Marcus, *Mark 1–8*, 426; similarly, Heil, *Jesus Walking on the Sea*, 70.

22 Several other OT passages echo this fundamental Exodus revelation in divine self-disclosure speeches, employing (in the LXX) the phrase ἐγώ εἰμι: e.g., Deut 32:39; Isa 41:4; 51:12; cf. Isa 43:11.

23 See chap. 3, below.

24 For a complex analysis of the problem of Jesus' divine identity in this passage, see Robert W. Jenson, "Jesus, Identity, and Exegesis," in Gaventa and Hays, *Seeking the Identity*, 43–59, esp. 51–59. Jenson defends a trinitarian reading of the passage.

25 For an evocative discussion of this theme, see Joel Marcus, "Identity and Ambiguity in Markan Christology," in Gaventa and Hays, *Seeking the Identity*, 133–47.

26 At the time of the delivery of this lecture in Cambridge, a questioner in the audience observed that the "non-identity" texts are chiefly found in utterances of Jesus, whereas the intimations of divine identity appear chiefly in Mark's third-person narration. What should we make of this undoubtedly correct observation? Once upon a time, NT criticism might have seized upon evidence of this sort to suggest that the Evangelist was superimposing a later "high" Christology on an earlier tradition of sayings material that represented a "lower" view of Jesus as a non-divine character. (The argument would run parallel to William Wrede's classic argument about Mark's imposition of a "messianic secret" on an originally non-messianic Jesus tradition.) Such a hypothesis, however, would have to posit an untenable view of Mark as a clumsy or incompetent author. Mark was perfectly capable, should he have chosen to do so, of selecting or creating sayings in which Jesus would affirm his divine identity (cf. John's Gospel)—or, even more to the point, suppressing "low" christological sayings that conflicted with his own preferred divine identity Christology. The Gospel narrative includes and embraces materials of both kinds, creating the paradoxical tension I have described in the text above. I would contend that, whatever the reasons might be for Mark's narrative strategy, the christological tension is integral to Mark's paradoxical theological vision. It should not be overlooked that this Gospel's claims about Jesus as the exalted Son of Man who will rule as *Kyrios* at God's right hand are also to be found only in the utterances of Jesus. Most importantly, Mark

has chosen to encode his proclamation of Jesus' divine identity chiefly through the device of figural narrative correspondence. (See the following section.) For that reason, it is not surprising that the hints of divine identity are to be found in authorial narration rather than in sayings material.

27 For a particularly clear illustration of this effect, see Richard A. Horsley, *Hearing the Whole Story: The Politics of Plot in Mark's Gospel* (Louisville, Ky.: Westminster John Knox, 2001).

28 The same emphasis on intentionality is found in the purpose clauses of Mark 4:21.

29 Several ancient scribes obviously felt similar unease about the sentence as Mark wrote it: several Greek manuscripts read ἅπτεται ("Is a lamp *lit* . . . ?"; D, W, *f*13, followed by some versions), but the more difficult reading ἔρχεται is clearly original. Interestingly, both Matthew and Luke also ameliorate the construction in different ways.

30 On this reading of the text, see Gathercole, *Preexistent Son*, 171–72 and references cited there. See also Lane, *Mark*, 165–66.

31 Notice that in Matthew, the component sentences of Mark 4:21-25 are strewn about in different places in the narrative: Matt 5:15; 10:26; 7:2; and 13:12. Needless to say, this passage creates complicated questions for source theories about the Synoptic Gospels.

32 The fuller context of the quotation is illuminating with regard to the present argument: "Poetry provides the one permissible way of saying one thing and meaning another. People say, 'Why don't you say what you mean?' We never do that, do we, being all of us too much poets. We like to talk in parables and in hints and in indirections—whether from diffidence or some other instinct" (Robert Frost, "Education by Poetry," speech delivered at Amherst College and subsequently revised for publication in the *Amherst Graduates' Quarterly* [February 1931]).

33 Frank Kermode, *The Genesis of Secrecy: On the Interpretation of Narrative* (Cambridge, Mass.: Harvard University Press, 1979), 47.

34 Rowan Williams, *Christ on Trial: How the Gospel Unsettles Our Judgement* (London: Fount, 2000), 6. Williams' imbedded quotation is from Anita Mason, *The Illusionist* (London: Abacus, 1983), 127, emphasis in original.

35 Doxastikon at the "Lord, I Have Cried," Vespers of St. Mark the Evangelist (April 25), with Greek text in TO MHNAION TOY AΠPIΛIOY (Athens: Saliberos, 1904), 102. I am grateful to John Chryssavgis for drawing this tradition to my attention and to George Parsenios for assistance with identifying the citation.

CHAPTER 3

1 Rowan Williams, *The Wound of Knowledge: A Theological History from the New Testament to Luther and St. John of the Cross* (Eugene, Ore.: Wipf & Stock, 1998), 1.

2 Williams, *Wound of Knowledge*, 3. Of course, the testimony of the Gospel writers is that the dead and condemned man Jesus was also raised triumphant from the dead. Williams' formulation, however, highlights the troubling, counterintuitive character of the early Christian proclamation of Jesus' death as a saving event.

3 Williams, *Wound of Knowledge*, 1.

4 I am mindful of the possible double sense of the word "enormity," and I use it here

intentionally to invoke that double sense. While in much contemporary usage "enormity" means simply "hugeness" or "immensity," its original root meaning is "extreme wickedness." From the perspective of many devout Jews in antiquity, the emergent early Christian identification of Jesus with the God of Israel would have been shocking or blasphemous. Thus, to speak of the enormity of the claims about Jesus is at once to recognize the transgressive character of the Evangelists' "reorganization of religious language" and to acknowledge their sweeping scope.

5   Paul S. Minear, *The Good News according to Matthew: A Training Manual for Prophets* (St. Louis: Chalice, 2000).

6   On the development and significance of the fourfold Gospel canon, see Graham N. Stanton, "The Fourfold Gospel," *NTS* 43 (1997): 317–46; idem, *The Gospels and Jesus*, 2nd ed. (New York: Oxford University Press, 2002). For a comprehensive, hermeneutically nuanced account, see Francis Watson, *Gospel Writing: A Canonical Perspective* (Grand Rapids: Eerdmans, 2013).

7   For an extensive bibliography of commentaries on Matthew prior to 1800, see Ulrich Luz, *Matthew 1–7: A Commentary* (Edinburgh: T&T Clark, 1989), 19–22.

8   Matt 1:22-23; 2:15, 17-18, 23; 4:14-16; 8:17; 12:17-21; 13:35; 21:4-5; and 27:9. Another quotation in this format appears in some late manuscripts at 27:35, but this has apparently been interpolated by later scribes, under the influence of John 19:24. It is perhaps noteworthy that all ten authentic Matthean formula quotations cite texts from the prophets, whereas the text cited in 27:35 is Ps 22:19, making the formulaic ἵνα πληρωθῇ τὸ ῥηθὲν διὰ τοῦ προφήτου not strictly appropriate. For discussion of these passages, see George M. Soares Prabhu, *The Formula Quotations in the Infancy Narrative of Matthew* (An Bib 63; Rome: Biblical Institute, 1976). The most detailed discussion of the text-form of Matthew's citations is now Menken, *Matthew's Bible*.

9   Matt 2:5-6; 3:3; and 13:14-15.

10 Donald Senior, "The Lure of the Formula Quotations: Re-assessing Matthew's Use of the Old Testament with the Passion Narrative as a Test Case," in *The Scriptures in the Gospels* (ed. Christopher Mark Tuckett; BETL 131; Leuven: Leuven University Press, 1997), 89–115, esp. 90.

11 Senior ("Lure," in Tuckett, *Scriptures in the Gospels*, 89) points out that "the Nestle-Aland appendix lists 294 implicit citations or allusions in Matthew."

12 Senior, "Lure," in Tuckett, *Scriptures in the Gospels*, 115.

13 For a detailed and methodologically elegant study of one of these narrative typologies, see Dale C. Allison Jr., *The New Moses: A Matthean Typology* (Minneapolis: Fortress, 1993). Likewise, for a fresh reading of Isaac typology in Matthew, see Leroy Huizenga, *The New Isaac: Tradition and Intertextuality in the Gospel of Matthew* (NovTSup 131; Leiden: Brill, 2009).

14 For a detailed study of this aspect of Matthean Christology, see David D. Kupp, *Matthew's Emmanuel: Divine Presence and God's People in the First Gospel* (SNTSMS 90; Cambridge: Cambridge University Press, 1996), 49–108.

15 For literature, see Luz, *Matthew 1–7*, 96.

16 My reflections about Matthew's identification of Jesus with Israel have been independently reinforced by an unpublished essay by Gaylen Leverett, "Jesus as Israel: A

Matthean Analogy." I am grateful to Dr. Leverett for sending this essay to me some years ago.

17 For purposes of the present discussion, it makes little difference whether Matthew was translating the Hebrew independently or following an extant Greek translation closer in wording to the MT. W. D. Davies and Dale C. Allison Jr. (*The Gospel according to Saint Matthew* [ICC; Edinburgh: T&T Clark, 1988], 1:262n8) mention that a scribal note in the margin of א ascribes Matthew's quotation to Num 24:8, which reads, in the LXX, "God led him out of Egypt." Given the widespread use of the oracle of Balaam as a messianic testimony (esp. Num 24:17), it is not surprising that early Christian readers, finding that the LXX of Hos 11:1 gave no support to Matthew's citation, would be drawn to Num 24:8 instead. Note also that Num 24:7 LXX reads, "A man shall come forth out of his [Israel's] seed, and he shall rule many nations." There is no evidence, however, that Matthew was aware of any of this. The suggestion of Davies and Allison (1:262) that Matthew's attention was drawn first to Numbers 24 and then secondarily to Hos 11:1 is speculative.

18 Davies and Allison (*Matthew*, 1:263–64) rightly identify this figural dimension of the story and see here a connection to other ancient Jewish sources that envision a new "eschatological exodus and return to the land."

19 Readers conversant with current debates in NT scholarship will recognize that the themes summarized here (Israel's return from exile, and Jesus as the one who enacts and leads the return) resonate strongly with the characteristic emphases of N. T. Wright's interpretation of Jesus' activity (*Jesus and the Victory of God*). Should such theological ideas be ascribed, as Wright argues, to Jesus' own conscious self-conception and purposes? Or do these ideas belong to the secondary level of Matthew's interpretation of the significance of Jesus? The latter is fairly certain, on the basis of explicit narrative features of Matthew's text. The former is a far more speculative matter.

20 Rightly noted by Christine Ritter, *Rachels Klage im antiken Judentum und frühen Christentum* (AGJU 52; Leiden: Brill, 2003), 121.

21 Ritter (*Rachels Klage*, 122–23) cautiously puts forward this suggestion.

22 What I am claiming here about Matthew is formally analogous to the finding of recent studies of Paul's readings of Israel's Scripture: Matthew, like Paul, sees a coherent *plot* in the OT texts that he cites. For Paul, see J. Ross Wagner, *Heralds of Salvation: Paul and Isaiah "In Concert" in Romans 9–11* (NovTSup 101; Leiden: Brill, 2002); Francis Watson, *Paul and the Hermeneutics of Faith* (London: T&T Clark, 2004).

23 In brief, "metalepsis," as analyzed by John Hollander, is a literary device that links two texts, A and B, in such a way that a fragmentary citation of A in B requires the reader to recall and supply elements of text A that are not explicitly cited. For fuller discussion of this literary device, see Hays, *Echoes of Scripture*.

24 Kupp (*Matthew's Emmanuel*, 226) surveys Matthew's uses of the term and draws an appropriate conclusion: "Beginning with the magi, [Matthew] builds an index of προσκυνήσις which starts with their perception of him as the divine child-king and elevates in the end to worship of the risen Jesus, the Emmanuel Messiah." I would add only that the climactic use of προσκυνεῖν in the resurrection appearance narrative retrospectively colors and informs its earlier occurrences.

25 The inference that Jesus is the "something greater" is strongly reinforced by the closely analogous assertions later in the same chapter that Jesus (along with his message?) is something greater than either Jonah or Solomon (Matt 12:41-42).

26 Jesus' presence as supplanting the Temple as locus of God's presence is explored by Kupp, *Matthew's Emmanuel*, 224–28.

27 For further discussion, see Kupp, *Matthew's Emmanuel*, 192–96. Without arguing for any literary dependence on *m.'Aboth* 3:2, Kupp suggests that the correspondence between the rabbinic saying and Matt 18:20 demonstrates a concern about God's presence which predates the Matthean saying. Davies and Allison (*Matthew*, 2:790) argue that the rabbinic parallels of Matt 18:20 were produced independently from the early Christian tradition.

28 Does the phrase "the least of these my brothers" refer comprehensively to all who are among the poor and suffering ones? Or should it be interpreted more restrictively to refer only to Jesus' disciples? The text has been read both ways in the Christian tradition. For an extensive study of the history of interpretation, see Sherman W. Gray, *The Least of My Brothers: Matthew 25:31-46, A History of Interpretation* (SBLDS 114; Atlanta: Scholars, 1989). Gray demonstrates that on balance the majority of Christian readings have favored the restrictive interpretation. Nonetheless, this meaning is far from explicit in the text, and the more generous, more universal reading continues to bubble up at many points in the tradition. For a defense of this broader reading, see Davies and Allison, *Matthew*, 3:428-30, citing support from exegetical worthies such as Gregory of Nyssa and John Chrysostom, along with a roster of modern commentators. The point I am making here about the presence of the Lord in the person of the poor does not depend strictly on a resolution of this exegetical problem.

29 The parallel is noted in Davies and Allison (*Matthew*, 3:430), with supporting references to Irenaeus and Clement of Alexandria. On the theme of "repayment" in Matthew, see Nathan Eubank, *Wages of Cross-Bearing and Debt of Sin: The Economy of Heaven in Matthew's Gospel* (BZNW 196; Berlin: de Gruyter, 2014).

30 On the Danielic Son of Man as sharer in the divine identity, see the discussion in the previous chapter on this theme in Mark's Gospel, pp. 18–19, above.

31 Kupp, *Matthew's Emmanuel*, 139.

32 If the distinction between the Father and the Son is to be understood as a distinction between God and not-God, then Matthew offers a wealth of material for an argument *against* Jesus' divine identity, for he develops the Father/Son language more fully than the other Synoptic Gospels. The purpose of this language in Matthew, however, is not to explicate claims or controversies about Jesus' "divinity": "Jesus both adopts and adapts the Old Testament presentation of God as the Father of Israel in speaking of himself as Son and of the community that he gathers together as his family. When Jesus speaks of God as Father, he does not primarily give expression to his own intuition or experience of God as near, loving, intimate, and accessible, nor does he intend first to articulate his own relationship to God." Marianne Meye Thompson, *The Promise of the Father: Jesus and God in the New Testament* (Louisville, Ky.: Westminster John Knox, 2000), 86. For an extended discussion, see R. W. L. Moberly, "Jesus in Matthew's Gospel as Son of God," in *The Bible, Theology, and*

Faith (Cambridge Studies in Christian Doctrine; Cambridge: Cambridge University Press, 2000), 184–224.

33   Within the scope of the present chapter, we have surveyed only a selection of the material that would support Matthew's theological tendency to highlight Jesus' divine identity. A fuller treatment could explore additional evidence. E.g., we could consider the antitheses of the Sermon on the Mount, in which Jesus not only radicalizes but even subverts or overrules the teaching of the Law of Moses—most strikingly in his refusal of the permission to divorce (5:31-32), his forbidding of oaths or vows (5:33-37), and his repudiation of the *lex talionis*, the retaliatory punishment of evildoers (5:38-41). Who has the authority to pronounce such revisionary judgments about the Law given to Moses? Surely only the one who was the original Lawgiver.

34   On Matthew's dialectical tensions, see Leander E. Keck, "Justification of the Ungodly and Ethics," in *Rechtfertigung* (ed. Johannes Friedrich, Wolfgang Pöhlmann, and Peter Stuhlmacher; Tübingen: Mohr Siebeck, 1984), 199–209; Richard B. Hays, *The Moral Vision of the New Testament: Community, Cross, New Creation* (New York: HarperCollins, 1996), 101–4, 107–9.

35   Kupp, *Matthew's Emmanuel*, 226–27.

Chapter 4

1   I discussed this text briefly in the opening lecture of this series in order to make the point that the NT teaches us to "read backwards" to find figural anticipations of Jesus Christ in the OT. I return to Luke 24 in the present lecture to explore more precisely *what* we will find when we do so.

2   See Hays, "Reading Scripture in Light of the Resurrection," in Davis and Hays, *Art of Reading Scripture*, 216–38.

3   Their account parallels the inadequate understanding of the crowds, as reported in Luke 9:19.

4   For a representative view, see, e.g., John Drury, "Luke, Gospel of," in *A Dictionary of Biblical Interpretation* (ed. R. J. Coggins and J. L. Houlden; London: SCM Press, 1990), 410–13: "It has long been noticed that [Luke] has a 'lower' christology than the other evangelists, and a much lower one than John." Similarly, Christopher M. Tuckett observes, "Many have argued that, insofar as Luke's views can be discerned, the picture is fundamentally a 'subordinationist' one: Jesus is presented as above all a human being who is subordinate to God" ("The Christology of Luke-Acts," in *The Unity of Luke-Acts* [ed. Joseph Verheyden; BETL 142; Leuven: Leuven University Press, 1999], 133–64, quotation from 148–49). Tuckett's characterization applies, *inter alia*, to the influential work of Hans Conzelmann, *The Theology of St Luke* (New York: Harper & Row, 1961; German original 1953, under the title *Die Mitte der Zeit*), 170–84. To be sure, there have been major monographs arguing instead for a "higher" Lukan Christology (notably Darrell Bock, *Proclamation from Prophecy and Pattern: Lucan Old Testament Christology* [JSNTSup 12; Sheffield: Sheffield Academic, 1987]; H. Douglas Buckwalter, *The Character and Purpose of Luke's Christology* [SNTSMS 89; Cambridge: Cambridge University Press, 1996]). But these have on the whole failed to sway the weight of critical opinion in the field (see Tuckett's critique in the Verheyden volume).

5 The classic influential statement of this view is C. F. D. Moule, "The Christology of Acts," in *Studies in Luke-Acts* (ed. Leander E. Keck and J. Louis Martyn; Nashville: Abingdon, 1966), 159–85.

6 As cogently articulated by Leander E. Keck, "Toward the Renewal of New Testament Christology," *NTS* 32 (1986): 362–77.

7 The paradigm-changing work that demonstrated the importance of *narrative* depiction of the identity of Jesus in the Gospels was Frei, *Identity of Jesus Christ*. For studies that pursue a narrative approach to interpreting Luke's Christology, see Rowe, *Early Narrative Christology*, esp. 17–23; Beverly R. Gaventa, "Learning and Relearning the Identity of Jesus from Luke-Acts," in Gaventa and Hays, *Seeking the Identity*, 148–65. On the general concept of "narrative identity," see especially Paul Ricoeur, *Oneself as Another* (Chicago: University of Chicago Press, 1992).

8 Richard Bauckham's proposal (*God Crucified*) that the study of NT Christology should focus on "divine identity" rather than ontological categories of divine essence has helpfully reshaped recent discussion of NT Christology.

9 Rowe, *Early Narrative Christology*.

10 Exceptions: Luke 2:23-24; 3:4-6.

11 As Robert L. Brawley observes, "The surface of Luke-Acts ripples with intertextuality because it constantly folds textual patterns from scripture into its text." Brawley, *Text to Text Pours Forth Speech: Voices of Scripture in Luke-Acts* (Bloomington: Indiana University Press, 1995), 3.

12 For further discussion of these themes in Luke-Acts, see Richard B. Hays, "Die Befreiung Israels im lukanischen Doppelwerk: Intertextuelle Erzählung als kulturkritische Praxis," in *Die Bibel im Dialog der Schriften: Konzepte Intertextueller Bibellektüre* (ed. Stefan Alkier and Richard B. Hays; Tübingen and Basel: Francke, 2005), 117–36; ET: "The Liberation of Israel in Luke-Acts: Intertextual Narration as Countercultural Practice," in Hays, Alkier, and Huizenga, *Reading the Bible Intertextually*, 101–17. For other approaches to the role of scriptural allusion in Luke's narrative, see Rebecca I. Denova, *The Things Accomplished among Us: Prophetic Tradition in the Structural Pattern of Luke-Acts* (JSNTSup 141; Sheffield: Sheffield Academic, 1997); Kenneth D. Litwak, *Echoes of Scripture in Luke-Acts: Telling the Story of God's People Intertextually* (JSNTSup 282; London: T&T Clark, 2005); Bock, *Proclamation from Prophecy and Pattern*.

13 Modern English translations (RSV, NRSV, NIV) characteristically overlook the force of the καί in the last line of Luke 1:35. I would suggest that here it means "also" and that it logically connects ἅγιον in this line to πνεῦμα ἅγιον at the beginning of the quotation from Gabriel. Thus: "The Holy Spirit will come upon you . . . therefore *also* [καί] the child to be born will be called *holy*."

14 In Luke 9:35, the textual tradition is divided between ὁ υἱός μου ὁ ἐκλελεγμένος and ὁ υἱός μου ὁ ἀγαπητός. The latter reading almost surely reflects scribal assimilation of the text to 3:22 as well as to the synoptic parallels in Mark 9:7 and Matt 17:5.

15 We should note also the climactic reference in Luke's genealogy to Adam as "son of God" (3:38). It is not just coincidental that the very next words in Luke are "But Jesus, full of the Holy Spirit" (4:1), and that the scene thus introduced is one in which the devil taunts Jesus with a challenge to prove that he is the Son of God. The

effect of this narrative technique is to link Jesus associatively with Adam. Adam is son of God because he is God's direct sovereign creation and has no human parents. It is possible that Luke is obliquely suggesting a christological identification of Jesus as the new Adam (cf. Rom 5:12-21). If so, however, this is not a theme that he develops elsewhere.

16 On this passage as a key indicator of Jesus' identity, see the interesting treatment in Joseph Ratzinger (Pope Benedict XVI), *Jesus of Nazareth: From the Baptism in the Jordan to the Transfiguration* (San Francisco: Ignatius Press, 2007), 339–45.

17 Even Luke's special emphasis on Jesus' intense disciplines of prayer (e.g., 3:21; 6:12; 9:18, 28-29; etc.) coheres with his affirmation in 10:22 of a specially intimate and mutual knowledge of God.

18 E. P. Sanders, *The Historical Figure of Jesus* (London: Penguin, 1993), 248: "A person who is above the judges of Israel is very high indeed."

19 For a recent survey of the evidence, see Adela Yarbro Collins and John J. Collins, *King and Messiah as Son of God: Divine, Human, and Angelic Messianic Figures in Biblical and Related Literature* (Grand Rapids: Eerdmans, 2008).

20 We should also observe that to proclaim Jesus as Son of God could well be heard as a politically provocative challenge to the authority of the Roman emperor, who also claimed precisely the title of υἱὸς θεοῦ.

21 David Pao, *Acts and the Isaianic New Exodus* (WUNT 2. Reihe 130; Tübingen: Mohr Siebeck, 2000; repr., Grand Rapids: Baker Academic, 2002), 38. Pao actually describes it as "*the* hermeneutical key" (emphasis added). For reasons that should be clear by now, I think it is methodologically mistaken to look for a single theme or image as the one key to Luke's narrative design. Nonetheless, my interpretation of the passage is significantly indebted to Pao's insightful exegetical work.

22 See my comments on Mark 1:2-3 in chap. 2, above (pp. 20–21). Luke's citation of Isa 40:3 agrees in its textual form with the citation found in Mark 1:3 and Matt 3:3. I regard it as certain that Luke drew on Mark as a source and probable that he drew on Matthew. Whatever theory of synoptic relationships one accepts, it is clear that Luke retains the ambiguity of the Markan form of the citation and enhances it not only through the longer citation of Isa 40:3-5 but also through his distinctive emphasis on κύριος as a title for Jesus.

23 Rowe, *Early Narrative Christology*, 70–74.

24 Rowe, *Early Narrative Christology*, 74–77.

25 By citing a fuller block of Isaiah 40, Luke merely gives the reader a more explicit prompt than does Mark to recognize the divine identity of Jesus. David Pao's analysis (*Isaianic New Exodus*, 147–80) argues that in the Acts of the Apostles the "Agent" of the new exodus is the word of God. But Pao does not focus the meaning of "word of God" in christological terms (as in the Johannine prologue). Rather, in terms of the Acts narrative, the word of God is the proclaimed message. But Luke 3:1-6 would suggest that however much the proclaimed message may have an instrumental role in implementing the new exodus, the true *agent* of the new exodus is Jesus the Lord himself. (This is also the implication of Acts 1:1.)

26 This tally does not count the vocative κύριε and other ambiguous instances.

27 These observations are simply a brief summary of C. Kavin Rowe's thorough,

theologically sophisticated analysis of this striking phenomenon in Luke's Gospel (*Early Narrative Christology*). For an earlier concise preview of his observations, see idem, "Luke and the Trinity: An Essay in Ecclesial Biblical Theology," *SJT* 56 (2003): 1–26.

28 For this reason, we cannot suppose that Acts 2:36 articulates an adoptionist Christology in which Jesus is "appointed" κύριος only at the time of the resurrection. Jesus has already been named as κύριος from the beginning of the two-volume work. As Rowe has shown, therefore, the climactic declaration of Peter's Pentecost sermon in Acts 2:36 should be understood to mean that as a result of the resurrection and the outpouring of the Spirit, all Israel should now *know* that God has appointed Jesus both Lord and Christ. The change effected by the resurrection is an epistemological one for the audience, not an ontological transformation or even a change of status for Jesus himself. C. Kavin Rowe, "Acts 2:36 and the Continuity of Lukan Christology," *NTS* 53 (2007): 37–56.

29 The manuscript evidence is divided on the inclusion or omission of the relative pronoun ὅν in this verse. With the inclusion of the relative pronoun in the text, the main verb of the clause would have to be οἴδατε in verse 37. The translation given here, however, follows ℵ¹ A B 81. 614. 1739 and a few other manuscripts in reading the verse without the pronoun; this has the effect of strengthening the affirmations in both clauses of verse 36. The reading with the pronoun requires that οὗτός ἐστιν πάντων κύριος be read as a parenthetical interjection. For purposes of the present argument, the sense of this clause is not materially affected. But narratively, it is hard to understand why Peter should (even rhetorically) treat the affirmations of verse 36 as something already known to his audience, and it is easy to see how the addition of ON could have arisen through dittography: ΤΟΝΛΟΓΟΝΟΝ.

30 Wilhelm Dittenberger, *Sylloge Inscriptionum Graecarum* (vol. 1; Hildesheim: Olms, 1960), 376.31.

31 Epictetus, *Discourse* 4.1.12.

32 See also Luke 18:41-43, for a similar response by a healed blind man. All of these examples are briefly noted by Rowe, *Early Narrative Christology*, 120–21n129.

33 Here, as elsewhere, the verb ἐπισκέπτομαι translates the Hebrew פקד, which has a wide range of meanings, including "look after, take care of."

34 On the importance of Psalm 80 in Jewish expressions of hope for God's intervention, see Andrew Streett, *The Vine and the Son of Man: Eschatological Interpretation of Psalm 80 in Early Judaism* (Minneapolis: Fortress, 2014).

35 Simon J. Gathercole, "The Heavenly ἀνατολή," *JSNT* 56 (2005): 471–88; idem, *Preexistent Son*, 238–42.

36 I am inclined to think that Luke's slight alteration of the main verb (το κατῃσχύνοντο) is meant for emphasis: as Isaiah prophesied that those who oppose the Lord would be put to shame (αἰσχυνθήσονται, future tense), so in fact those who oppose Jesus were *thoroughly* put to shame (κατῃσχύνοντο, imperfect tense). The prefix κατ- indicates that the shaming was decisive.

37 See the discussion of this theme in chap. 3, above (pp. 44–45).

38 Of course, traditional models of historical criticism might propose slightly more complex versions of the third possibility. E.g., it could be suggested that Luke is using

different hypothetical sources that he has not successfully molded into a theological unity. This is not in any significant way different from saying that he is a confused narrator. Alternatively, someone might propose that either Luke 4:8 or 24:52 has been added to the original text of Luke's Gospel by a later redactor or scribe. But there is no textual evidence for such a conjecture (i.e., an ancient manuscript of Luke lacking one or the other of these verses). And in any case such a conjecture would merely move the locus of confusion from some imagined "proto-Luke" to the final compiler of the canonical text. Thus, I would stand by my sketch of three basic possibilities.

39 In the Acts of the Apostles, the pressure of the text continues to move the reader in a similar direction. There, in Peter's Pentecost sermon, we encounter a citation of Joel 3:5 LXX (= 2:32 in most English translations): "[E]veryone who calls on the name of the Lord shall be saved" (Acts 2:21). As Luke's account unfolds, we learn in no uncertain terms that "the Lord" is Jesus (2:36; cf. "the Lord our God" in 2:39), that those who believe Peter's message are to be baptized in the name of Jesus (2:38), and that there is "no other name" given by which human beings can be saved (4:12). The reader who connects the dots between Joel's prophecy and Peter's speeches can hardly avoid the implication that Luke is implying/proclaiming the divine identity of Jesus as Lord.

40 Much of the evidence we have considered in this chapter is distinctive to Luke's Gospel. The logion in Luke 13:34, however, has a very close parallel in Matt 23:37. Depending on one's theory of synoptic relationships, this would mean either that the passage is a Q text or that Luke has derived it from Matthew. In either case, within the context of Luke's narrative, the saying reinforces the pattern we have already seen consistently developed by Luke. He has appropriated this logion, from whatever source, into a narrative that intimates Jesus' divine identity.

41 See also Isa 31:5, a relevant but slightly more ambiguous text.

42 If Luke 13:34 were taken in isolation as a traditional logion, it could perhaps be interpreted as an instance of prophetic speech, in which the prophet speaks in the first person as a mouthpiece for God. But Luke has narratively contextualized the saying as Jesus' own speech and placed it within a narrative that, as we have seen, contains numerous other indications that Jesus speaks not on behalf of God but as the embodied presence of God. This is a good illustration of the importance of reading the narrative whole and seeing how the identity of Jesus is depicted within Luke's story rather than in a hypothetical earlier source.

43 This example illustrates that a consistent Moses typology breaks down under the logic of Luke's narration: Jesus is cast here not as the Moses figure who will be given words to testify but rather as the Lord who is the giver of powerful speech. Note that in the very similar commissioning promise of Luke 12:11-12, it is the Holy Spirit who will teach the disciples what to say when they are hauled up before hostile authorities.

44 Max Turner, "'Trinitarian' Pneumatology in the New Testament? Towards an Explanation of the Worship of Jesus," *AsTJ* 57 (2002): 167–86.

45 These passages are cited as translated from the MT by the NRSV. The LXX renderings differ in significant respects, but all agree in referring to God as the Redeemer of Israel. I have cited in brackets the relevant divine titles as they appear in the LXX. In all four passages, the Hebrew word translated as "Redeemer" is גֹּאֵל.

Chapter 5

1   Mishnah *Šabb.* 7:2 lists thirty-nine classes of work prohibited on the sabbath. The
     last item in the list is "taking out aught from one domain to another." John P. Meier
     ("The Historical Jesus and the Historical Sabbath," in *Redefining First-Century Jew-
     ish and Christian Identities: Essays in Honor of Ed Parish Sanders* [ed. Fabian Udoh
     et al.; Notre Dame, Ind.: University of Notre Dame Press, 2008], 297–307), on
     form-critical grounds, dismisses this story, as well as the healing story in John 9, as
     valid *historical* evidence about controversy surrounding Jesus' healing on the sabbath
     (302–3). He then notes, almost as an afterthought, that John 5 focuses the contro-
     versy not on the act of healing but on the prohibited carrying of a burden, but he
     regards this as a late, secondary addendum to the tradition that "tries to make the
     sabbath disputes more plausible" (307n15). To the contrary, the possibility should
     at least be considered that John 5:9-10 preserves an early tradition that explains why
     Jesus' sabbath healing activity was controversial in the first place, despite the absence
     of a scriptural basis for prohibition of healing on the sabbath. In any case, the his-
     torical antiquity and reliability of the tradition behind John's narrative is immaterial
     for the questions at hand in my discussion. Within the narrative world of John 5,
     the controversy focuses on the prohibited carrying of a burden, and it morphs into a
     larger dispute and discourse about Jesus' relation to the Father.

2   C. K. Barrett, "The Old Testament in the Fourth Gospel," *JTS* 48 (1947): 155–69;
     the reference to Westcott and Hort is on p. 155.

3   See, e.g., Bruce G. Schuchard, *Scripture within Scripture: The Interrelationship of Form
     and Function in the Explicit Old Testament Citations in the Gospel of John* (SBLDS 133;
     Atlanta: Scholars, 1992), xiii–xiv (13 quotations); Andreas Köstenberger, "John,"
     in *Commentary on the New Testament Use of the Old Testament* (ed. G. K. Beale and
     D. A. Carson; Grand Rapids: Baker Academic, 2007), 415–21 (14 quotations); Mar-
     garet Daly-Denton, *David in the Fourth Gospel: The Johannine Reception of the Psalms*
     (AGJU 47; Leiden: Brill, 2000), 33–34 (16 quotations); Menken, *Old Testament
     Quotations*, 11–12 (17 quotations).

4   Margaret Daly-Denton (*David in the Fourth Gospel*, 30) describes overt allusions in
     the Fourth Gospel as "quite rare" and suggests there are only two that would meet
     strict criteria for identifying allusions: "the reference to the angels ascending and
     descending on the Son of Man (2:51 [*sic*, read 1:51 instead], alluding to Gen 28:12)
     and the speculation of the crowd that the Christ is to be of the seed of David and is to
     come from Bethlehem (7:42, alluding to 2 Sam 7:12 and Ps [88]89:3-4)." This judg-
     ment surely results from an excessively stringent definition of what constitutes an
     allusion. By contrast, Andreas Köstenberger ("John," in Beale and Carson, *Commen-
     tary*, 419–20) lists more than sixty "Old Testament allusions and verbal parallels" in
     the Gospel, in addition to the explicit quotations. Daly-Denton is of course aware of
     the much richer intertextual character of John's Gospel. She goes on to say that "the
     apparent infrequency of Scripture reference in the Fourth Gospel is quite deceptive,"
     and she acknowledges the "highly allusive quality of [John's] writing" (30).

5   The phrase "in the wilderness" also appears earlier in the Numbers passage, not
     in relation to Moses' action of lifting up the serpent, but as part of the people's

complaint: "Why have you brought us out of Egypt to kill us in the wilderness?" (Num 21:5 LXX).

6 In John 19:28, the formula ἵνα τελειωθῇ ἡ γραφή ("in order that the scripture might be brought to completion") introduces a word of Jesus but not a direct scriptural quotation. John's poetic purpose in selecting this distinctive wording in just this place in the story will be discussed below.

7 The latter designation requires comment. The titles "Book of Signs" and "Book of Glory" were proposed by Raymond Brown in his excellent and highly influential Anchor Bible commentary on the Fourth Gospel (*The Gospel according to John* [AB 29 and 29A; Garden City, N.Y.: Doubleday, 1966, 1970]). Brown's analysis included chap. 20 as part of the Book of Glory (13:1–20:31), with chap. 21 seen as an epilogue added at a later redactional stage. The term "book of the passion," adopted above, was suggested earlier by C. H. Dodd (*The Interpretation of the Fourth Gospel* [Cambridge: Cambridge University Press, 1953]); this terminology is preferred, rightly in my judgment, by Marianne Meye Thompson ("'They Bear Witness to Me': The Psalms in the Passion Narrative of the Gospel of John," in Ross, Rowe, and Grieb, *Word Leaps the Gap*, 267–83), to whom I owe the important observation of the structural role of the paired quotations in 12:38-40 and 19:36-37. If we follow these pairings as structural clues to the narrative, we will then see the second major section ending at the end of chap. 19, with chaps. 20–21 constituting a final separate narrative unit (a "book of resurrection"?). For a strong argument that John 21 belongs to the original narrative design of the Gospel, see Paul S. Minear, "The Original Functions of John 21," *JBL* 102 (1983): 85–98. Other supporters of this view are cited in Beverly R. Gaventa, "The Archive of Excess: John 21 and the Problem of Narrative Closure," in *Exploring the Gospel of John: In Honor of D. Moody Smith* (ed. R. Alan Culpepper and C. Clifton Black; Louisville, Ky.: Westminster John Knox, 1996), 240–55. For a very different argument in favor of seeing John 21 as part of the Gospel's design, based on a complex theory of numerical composition, see now Richard Bauckham, *The Testimony of the Beloved Disciple: Narrative, History, and Theology in the Gospel of John* (Grand Rapids: Baker Academic, 2007), 271–84.

8 Interestingly, there are no direct scriptural quotations in the Gospel's well-developed account of the resurrection (chaps. 20 and 21).

9 My translation "*persistently* did not believe" seeks to emphasize the force of the imperfect tense verb ἐπίστευον.

10 Marianne Meye Thompson comments: "Taken together, the scriptures cited in 12:38–19:42 bear witness . . . to Jesus' rejection, as do the quotations from Isaiah that summarize the predominantly negative response to Jesus' signs. The belief that Scripture testifies to Jesus' identity as Israel's Messiah lies behind those texts, but the actual quotations foreground the negative response to him. It is Israel's unbelief, the rejection of Jesus by 'his own' (1:11), that particularly troubles the evangelist and demands a scriptural explanation." Thompson, "They Bear Witness," in Wagner, Rowe, and Grieb, *Word Leaps the Gap*, 268.

11 See the discussion of the Matthean evidence in chap. 3, pp. 37–43, above.

12 Her chart actually says 76 percent, but this appears to be a computational error because her immediately preceding text states that "the Psalter is the source for ten

of the sixteen quotations found in the Fourth Gospel." Her contrasting figures for
the Synoptics are the following: Mark, 21 percent; Matthew, 18 percent; Luke, 31
percent (Daly-Denton, *David in the Fourth Gospel*, 34). I would conjecture that the
figure of 76 percent is derived in the following way: Daly-Denton notes that John
has thirteen "readily identifiable" Scripture quotations, of which seven derive from
the Psalms. She then notes that there are three more citations that do not fully correspond to any known Scripture passages, all of which she regards as "non literal
quotations from the psalms." It would seem that for the purposes of her statistical
analysis, she has added these three quotations to the numerator but not the denomi-
nator of her tabulation of Johannine quotations: this would yield ten out of thirteen,
or 76.9 percent. All these percentages, of course, might vary with different ways of
counting and attributing the quotations. But on any reckoning of the statistics, it is
difficult to quarrel with Köstenberger's judgment that for John, "the OT theological
center, at least as far as explicit OT quotations are concerned, is clearly the Psalter"
("John," in Beale and Carson, *Commentary*, 419).

13 See Richard B. Hays, "Christ Prays the Psalms: Israel's Psalter as Matrix of Early
    Christology," in *Conversion of the Imagination*, 101–18. I have proposed that the
    Psalms of suffering and vindication were the generative matrix for the early Chris-
    tian conviction that the death and resurrection of Jesus occurred "according to the
    Scriptures." The evidence of John's Gospel is entirely consistent with this thesis.

14 For discussion of the textual source of this quotation, see Menken, *Old Testament
    Quotations*, 147–66. Menken concludes that Ps 33:21 LXX provides "the basic text"
    and that the Pentateuchal texts "supplied the material for changes in it" (165).

15 For discussion, see Brown, *John*, 16.

16 See Mary L. Coloe, *God Dwells with Us: Temple Symbolism in the Fourth Gospel* (Col-
    legeville, Minn.: Liturgical Press, 2001); Alan R. Kerr, *The Temple of Jesus' Body: The
    Temple Theme in the Gospel of John* (JSNTSup 220; London: Sheffield Academic,
    2002).

17 Cf. Wis 8:4: "She is an initiate in the knowledge of God, and an associate in his
    works." Or again, Wis 9:9: "With you is Wisdom, she who knows your works and
    was present when you made the world."

18 Translation from F. H. Colson and G. H. Whittaker, *Philo*, vol. 4 (LCL; Cambridge,
    Mass.: Harvard University Press, 1932; London: Heinemann, 1932), 385. I have
    taken the liberty of replacing the English "Word" with the transliterated Greek
    word "*Logos*."

19 On this analysis of the Johannine prologue, see Boyarin, "Gospel of the *Memra*";
    idem, *Border Lines*, 89–111.

20 Richard Bauckham has emphasized that within Israel's Scripture the work of cre-
    ation of the world is solely to be attributed to the action of the one God of Israel
    (*Jesus and the God of Israel*, 7–11). Within this theological framework, references
    to the role of Wisdom in creation of the world must be understood as the poetic
    personification of a divine attribute, not as the name of a created entity.

21 John's citation of Ps 69:9 (LXX Ps 68:10) has shifted the verb tense from the aorist
    form in the LXX (κατέφαγεν) to the future tense form (καταφάγεται), thus facilitating
    its interpretation as a prefiguration of Jesus' action.

22 The observations on John 2 summarized here were developed more fully in my earlier essay "Reading Scripture in Light of the Resurrection," in Davis and Hays, *Art of Reading Scripture*, 216–38; see esp. 221–24.

23 John's christological reading of the Psalms, particularly the psalms of lament, is entirely consonant with other important streams of tradition in early Christianity. For other readings of Psalm 69 as speech of the Messiah, see Rom 15:3; Matt 27:48; Mark 15:36; Luke 23:36; John 19:29. On the whole question, see Richard B. Hays, "Christ Prays the Psalms," in *Conversion of the Imagination*, 101–18.

24 Once again, I would insist that the retrospective interpretation of an OT text as a figural precursor of a subsequent person or event does not deny or negate the historical reality of the precursor. Both the OT type and the NT antitype stand together as concrete disclosures of God's activity in the world. Therefore, the hermeneutical current flows in both directions, and the "meaning" of each pole in the typological correlation is enhanced by its relation to the other. See the discussion of figural reading and typology in chap. 1 of the present work.

25 For an exposition of the pervasive allusions to the Temple motif in John, see Ulrich Busse, "Die Tempelmetaphorik als ein Beispiel von implizitem Rekurs auf die biblische Tradition im Johannesevangelium," in Tuckett, *Scriptures in the Gospels*, 395–428.

26 See Seth Klayman, "Sukkoth from the Tanakh to Tannaitic Texts: Exegetical Traditions, Emergent Rituals, and Eschatological Associations" (Ph.D. diss., Duke University, 2008).

27 The vivid verb ἔκραξεν draws the reader's attention to the dramatic public character of Jesus' declaration.

28 T. S. Eliot, "The Dry Salvages," in *The Complete Poems and Plays* (New York: Harcourt, Brace & World, 1962), 133.

29 The verbal link is even closer to Ps 78:24, a retelling of the same story.

CHAPTER 6

1 The reader should take careful note of the construction of this sentence: "not only . . . but also." I am proposing not the rejection of modern critical readings but a corrective and enrichment.

2 For exposition of Auerbach's understanding of figural interpretation, see chap. 1 above and the sources cited there.

3 Jeremy Begbie, "Listening to the St. Luke Passion," program notes for U.S. premiere of James MacMillan's *Saint Luke Passion*, Duke Chapel, Durham, N.C., April 13, 2014.

4 That trap of epistemological smugness is not likely to be a danger for a suffering minority community such as the community of Mark's likely original readers. But for those who stand in more privileged social locations, the warning is not superfluous.

5 See Irenaeus, *Against Heresies* I.viii.5; I.ix.1–3; III.xi.7.

6 The triennial lectionary cycle represents one discipline of interpretation that would attempt to do justice to each synoptic witness.

7 In the course of my study of Matthew's scriptural hermeneutic, I have come to a much deeper appreciation for his carefulness and sophistication as an interpreter.

But I remain somewhat perplexed by his apparent lack of symbolic/systematic consistency.

8   After hearing me offer this analogy during the course of delivering the Hulseans, Professor Morna Hooker commented that she had recently given a talk on allusions to Scripture in Charles Wesley's hymns—only to discover that her audience was largely unfamiliar with both and therefore somewhat mystified by her lecture. I fear that a similar problem often attends the church's comprehension of the Old Testament in the New.

9   Arthur Miller, quoted by Richard Eyre in his director's notes for the *Playbill* for the Broadway production of *The Crucible*, 2001.

10   See thesis number four in "Nine Theses on the Interpretation of Scripture," in Davis and Hays, *Art of Reading Scripture*, 2–3.

11   See Richard Bauckham, "Reading Scripture as a Coherent Story," in Davis and Hays, *Art of Reading Scripture*, 38–53; cf. also thesis number two on pp. 1–2 of the same volume.

12   See, e.g., Luke Timothy Johnson, *Septuagintal Midrash in the Speeches of Acts* (Milwaukee: Marquette University Press, 2002); and David P. Moessner, "Luke's 'Plan of God' from the Greek Psalter: The Rhetorical Thrust of 'the Prophets and the Psalms' in Peter's Speech at Pentecost," in *Scripture and Traditions: Essays on Early Judaism and Christianity in Honor of Carl R. Holladay* (ed. Patrick Gray and Gail R. O'Day; NovTSup 129; Leiden: Brill, 2008), 223–38; idem, "'Abraham Saw My Day': Making Greater Sense of John 8:48-59 from the LXX Version than the MT Genesis 22," in *Die Septuaginta und das frühe Christentum* (ed. Thomas S. Caulley and Hermann Lichtenberger; Tübingen: Mohr Siebeck, 2011), 329–38. For historical background to the question, see Martin Hengel, *The Septuagint as Christian Scripture: Its Prehistory and the Problem of Its Canon* (OTS; Edinburgh: T&T Clark, 2002); and J. Ross Wagner, *Reading the Sealed Book: Old Greek Isaiah and the Problem of Septuagint Hermeneutics* (FAT 88; Tübingen: Mohr Siebeck; Waco, Tex.: Baylor University Press, 2013).

13   Bart D. Ehrman, *Jesus, Interrupted: Revealing the Hidden Contradictions in the Bible (and Why We Don't Know about Them)* (New York: HarperCollins, 2009), 249. See also his most recent popularization of this familiar claim: Bart D. Ehrman, *How Jesus Became God: The Exaltation of a Jewish Preacher from Galilee* (New York: HarperOne, 2014).

14   One classic statement of such a view is Wilhelm Bousset, *Kyrios Christos: Geschichte des Christusglaubens von den Anfangen des Christentums bis Irenaeus* (Göttingen: Vandenhoeck & Ruprecht, 1913; rev. ed., 1921); ET: *Kyrios Christos: A History of the Belief in Christ from the Beginnings of Christianity to Irenaeus* (Nashville: Abingdon, 1970; repr., Waco, Tex.: Baylor University Press, 2013). For a concise critique of some of the problems with Bousset's account, see Hurtado, *Lord Jesus Christ*, 19–24.

15   Once again, I would draw the reader's attention to the important work of Richard Bauckham, *Jesus and the God of Israel*.

16   Karl Barth, *Church Dogmatics* IV/1 (Edinburgh: T&T Clark, 1956), 186.

Works Cited

Alkier, Stefan. "Intertextuality and the Semiotics of Biblical Texts." In Hays, Alkier, and Huizenga, *Reading the Bible Intertextually*, 3–21.

Allison, Dale C., Jr. *The New Moses: A Matthean Typology*. Minneapolis: Fortress, 1993.

Auerbach, Erich. "Figura." In *Time, History, and Literature: Selected Essays of Erich Auerbach*, edited by James I. Porter, translated by Jane O. Newman, 65–113. Princeton: Princeton University Press, 2014.

———. *Mimesis*. Princeton: Princeton University Press, 1968.

Barrett, C. K. "The Old Testament in the Fourth Gospel." *Journal of Theological Studies* 48 (1947): 155–69.

Barth, Karl. *Church Dogmatics* IV/1. Edinburgh: T&T Clark, 1956.

Bauckham, Richard. *God Crucified: Monotheism and Christology in the New Testament*. Grand Rapids: Eerdmans, 1999.

———. *Jesus and the God of Israel: God Crucified and Other Studies on the New Testament's Christology of Divine Identity*. Grand Rapids: Eerdmans, 2008.

———. "Reading Scripture as a Coherent Story." In Davis and Hays, *Art of Reading Scripture*, 38–53.

———. *The Testimony of the Beloved Disciple: Narrative, History, and Theology in the Gospel of John*. Grand Rapids: Baker Academic, 2007.

Begbie, Jeremy. "Listening to the St. Luke Passion." Program notes for U.S. premiere of James MacMillan's *Saint Luke Passion*, Duke Chapel, Durham, N.C., April 13, 2014.

Bock, Darrell. *Proclamation from Prophecy and Pattern: Lucan Old Testament Christology*. Journal for the Study of the New Testament: Supplement Series 12. Sheffield: Sheffield Academic, 1987.

Bockmuehl, Markus. *Seeing the Word: Refocusing New Testament Study*. Grand Rapids: Baker Academic, 2006.

Bonhoeffer, Dietrich. *Widerstand und Ergebung: Briefe und Aufzeichnungen aus der Haft.* Edited by Christian Gremmels, Eberhard Bethge, and Renata Bethge, in collaboration with Ilse Tödt. Gütersloh: Chr. Kaiser, 1998.

Bousset, Wilhelm. *Kyrios Christos: Geschichte des Christusglaubens von den Anfangen des Christentums bis Irenaeus.* Göttingen: Vandenhoeck & Ruprecht, 1913. Rev. ed., 1921. ET: *Kyrios Christos: A History of the Belief in Christ from the Beginnings of Christianity to Irenaeus.* Nashville: Abingdon, 1970. Reprint, Waco, Tex.: Baylor University Press, 2013.

Boyarin, Daniel. *Border Lines: The Partition of Judaeo-Christianity.* Philadelphia: University of Pennsylvania Press, 2004.

———. "The Gospel of the *Memra*: Jewish Binitarianism and the Prologue to John." *Harvard Theological Review* 94 (2001): 243–84.

———. *The Jewish Gospels: The Story of the Jewish Christ.* New York: New Press, 2011.

Brawley, Robert L. *Text to Text Pours Forth Speech: Voices of Scripture in Luke-Acts.* Bloomington: Indiana University Press, 1995.

Brown, Raymond. *The Gospel according to John.* Anchor Bible 29 and 29A. Garden City, N.Y.: Doubleday, 1966, 1970.

Buckwalter, H. Douglas. *The Character and Purpose of Luke's Christology.* Society for New Testament Studies Monograph Series 89. Cambridge: Cambridge University Press, 1996.

Bultmann, Rudolf. *History of the Synoptic Tradition.* New York: Harper & Row, 1963.

Busse, Ulrich. "Die Tempelmetaphorik als ein Beispiel von implizitem Rekurs auf die biblische Tradition im Johannesevangelium." In Tuckett, *Scriptures in the Gospels,* 395–428.

Collins, Adela Yarbro, and John J. Collins. *King and Messiah as Son of God: Divine, Human, and Angelic Messianic Figures in Biblical and Related Literature.* Grand Rapids: Eerdmans, 2008.

Coloe, Mary L. *God Dwells with Us: Temple Symbolism in the Fourth Gospel.* Collegeville, Minn.: Liturgical Press, 2001.

Colson, F. H., and G. H. Whittaker. *Philo.* Vol. 4. Loeb Classical Library. Cambridge, Mass.: Harvard University Press, 1932; London: Heinemann, 1932.

Conzelmann, Hans. *The Theology of St Luke.* New York: Harper & Row, 1961. German original 1953, under the title *Die Mitte der Zeit.*

Dahl, Nils A. *Jesus the Christ: The Historical Origins of Christian Doctrine.* Edited by Donald Juel. Minneapolis: Fortress, 1991.

Daly-Denton, Margaret. *David in the Fourth Gospel: The Johannine Reception of the Psalms.* Arbeiten zur Geschichte des antiken Judentums und des Urchristentums 47. Leiden: Brill, 2000.

Davies, W. D., and Dale C. Allison Jr. *The Gospel according to Saint Matthew*. 3 vols. International Critical Commentary. Edinburgh: T&T Clark, 1988.

Davis, Ellen F., and Richard B. Hays, eds. *The Art of Reading Scripture*. Grand Rapids: Eerdmans, 2003.

Denova, Rebecca I. *The Things Accomplished among Us: Prophetic Tradition in the Structural Pattern of Luke-Acts*. Journal for the Study of the New Testament: Supplement Series 141. Sheffield: Sheffield Academic, 1997.

Dittenberger, Wilhelm. *Sylloge Inscriptionum Graecarum*. Vol. 1. Hildesheim: Olms, 1960.

Dodd, C. H. *According to the Scriptures: The Sub-structure of New Testament Theology*. London: Nisbet, 1952.

———. *The Interpretation of the Fourth Gospel*. Cambridge: Cambridge University Press, 1953.

Drury, John. "Luke, Gospel of." In *A Dictionary of Biblical Interpretation*, edited by R. J. Coggins and J. L. Houlden. London: SCM Press, 1990.

Ehrman, Bart D. *How Jesus Became God: The Exaltation of a Jewish Preacher from Galilee*. New York: HarperOne, 2014.

———. *Jesus, Interrupted: Revealing the Hidden Contradictions in the Bible (and Why We Don't Know about Them)*. New York: HarperCollins, 2009.

Eliot, T. S. "The Dry Salvages." In *The Complete Poems and Plays*. New York: Harcourt, Brace & World, 1962.

Epictetus. *The Discourses of Epictetus*. Translated by P. E. Mathison. Oxford: Clarendon, 1916.

Esler, Philip F. "The Incident of the Withered Fig Tree in Mark 11: A New Source and Redactional Explanation." *Journal for the Study of the New Testament* 28 (2005): 41–67.

Eubank, Nathan. *Wages of Cross-Bearing and Debt of Sin: The Economy of Heaven in Matthew's Gospel*. Beihefte zur Zeitschrift für die neutestamentliche Wissenschaft 196. Berlin: de Gruyter, 2014.

Evans, C. F. *Saint Luke*. TPI New Testament Commentaries. London: SCM Press, 1990.

Frei, Hans W. *The Eclipse of Biblical Narrative: A Study in Eighteenth and Nineteenth Century Hermeneutics*. New Haven: Yale University Press, 1974.

———. *The Identity of Jesus Christ: The Hermeneutical Bases of Dogmatic Theology*. Philadelphia: Fortress, 1975.

Frost, Robert. "Education by Poetry." Speech delivered at Amherst College and subsequently revised for publication in the *Amherst Graduates' Quarterly*, February 1931.

Funk, Robert W., Roy W. Hoover, et al. *The Five Gospels*. New York: Macmillan, 1993.

Gathercole, Simon. "The Heavenly ἀνατολή." *Journal for the Study of the New Testament* 56 (2005): 471–88.

———. *The Preexistent Son: Recovering the Christologies of Matthew, Mark, and Luke.* Grand Rapids: Eerdmans, 2006.

Gaventa, Beverly R. "The Archive of Excess: John 21 and the Problem of Narrative Closure." In *Exploring the Gospel of John: In Honor of D. Moody Smith,* edited by R. Alan Culpepper and C. Clifton Black, 240–55. Louisville, Ky.: Westminster John Knox, 1996.

———. "Learning and Relearning the Identity of Jesus from Luke-Acts." In Gaventa and Hays, *Seeking the Identity,* 148–65.

Gaventa, Beverly R., and Richard B. Hays, eds. *Seeking the Identity of Jesus: A Pilgrimage.* Grand Rapids: Eerdmans, 2008.

Goodacre, Mark. *The Case against Q: Studies in Markan Priority and the Synoptic Problem.* Harrisburg, Pa.: Trinity International, 2002.

———. "The Evangelists' Use of the Old Testament and the Synoptic Problem." In *New Studies in the Synoptic Problem: Oxford Conference, April 2008; Essays in Honour of Christopher M. Tuckett,* edited by P. Foster, A. Gregory, J. S. Kloppenborg, and J. Verheyden, 281–98. Bibliotheca ephemeridum theologicarum lovaniensium 239. Leuven: Peeters, 2011.

———. *Thomas and the Gospels: The Case for Thomas's Familiarity with the Synoptics.* Grand Rapids: Eerdmans, 2012.

Gray, Sherman W. *The Least of My Brothers: Matthew 25:31-46, A History of Interpretation.* Society of Biblical Literature Dissertation Series 114. Atlanta: Scholars, 1989.

Hays, Christopher B. *Death in the Iron Age II and in 1 Isaiah.* Forschungen zum Alten Testament 79. Tübingen: Mohr Siebeck, 2011.

———. "Echoes of the Ancient Near East? Intertextuality and the Comparative Study of the Old Testament." In Wagner, Rowe, and Grieb, *Word Leaps the Gap,* 20–43.

Hays, Richard B. *The Conversion of the Imagination: Paul as Interpreter of Israel's Scripture.* Grand Rapids: Eerdmans, 2005. See esp. "Christ Prays the Psalms: Israel's Psalter as Matrix of Early Christology"; and "'Who Has Believed Our Message?' Paul's Reading of Isaiah."

———. "Die Befreiung Israels im lukanischen Doppelwerk: Intertextuelle Erzählung als kulturkritische Praxis." In *Die Bibel im Dialog der Schriften: Konzepte Intertextueller Bibellektüre,* edited by Stefan Alkier and Richard B. Hays, 117–36. Tübingen and Basel: Francke, 2005. ET: "The Liberation of Israel in Luke-Acts: Intertextual Narration as Countercultural Practice." In Hays, Alkier, and Huizenga, *Reading the Bible Intertextually,* 101–17.

———. *Echoes of Scripture in the Letters of Paul*. New Haven: Yale University Press, 1989.

———. *The Moral Vision of the New Testament: Community, Cross, New Creation*. New York: HarperCollins, 1996.

———. "Reading Scripture in Light of the Resurrection." In Davis and Hays, *Art of Reading Scripture*, 216–38.

Hays, Richard B., Stefan Alkier, and Leroy A. Huizenga, eds. *Reading the Bible Intertextually*. Waco, Tex.: Baylor University Press, 2009.

Heil, J. P. *Jesus Walking on the Sea: Meaning and Gospel Functions of Matt 14:22-33, Mark 6:45-52, and John 6:15b-21*. Analecta Biblica 87. Rome: Pontifical Institute, 1981.

Hengel, Martin. *Between Jesus and Paul: Studies in the Earliest History of Christianity*. Philadelphia: Fortress, 1983. Reprint, Waco, Tex.: Baylor University Press, 2013.

———. *The Septuagint as Christian Scripture: Its Prehistory and the Problem of Its Canon*. Old Testament Studies. Edinburgh: T&T Clark, 2002.

Hooker, Morna D. *The Gospel according to Saint Mark*. Black's New Testament Commentary. London: A&C Black, 1991.

Horsley, Richard A. *Hearing the Whole Story: The Politics of Plot in Mark's Gospel*. Louisville, Ky.: Westminster John Knox, 2001.

Huizenga, Leroy. *The New Isaac: Tradition and Intertextuality in the Gospel of Matthew*. Supplements to Novum Testamentum 131. Leiden: Brill, 2009.

Hurtado, Larry. *Lord Jesus Christ: Devotion to Jesus in Earliest Christianity*. Grand Rapids: Eerdmans, 2003.

———. *One God, One Lord: Early Christian Devotion and Ancient Jewish Monotheism*. Edinburgh: T&T Clark, 1988.

Irenaeus. *Against Heresies*. In *Ante-Nicene Fathers: Volume 1, The Apostolic Fathers, Justin Martyr, Irenaeus*. Edited by Alexander Roberts and James Donaldson, revised by A. Cleveland Coxe, 315–567. Peabody, Mass.: Hendrickson, 1999.

Jenson, Robert W. "Jesus, Identity, and Exegesis." In Gaventa and Hays, *Seeking the Identity*, 43–59.

Johnson, Luke Timothy. *Septuagintal Midrash in the Speeches of Acts*. Milwaukee: Marquette University Press, 2002.

Juel, Donald. *Messianic Exegesis: Christological Interpretation of the Old Testament in Early Christianity*. Philadelphia: Fortress, 1988.

Keck, Leander E. "Justification of the Ungodly and Ethics." In *Rechtfertigung*, edited by Johannes Friedrich, Wolfgang Pöhlmann, and Peter Stuhlmacher, 199–209. Tübingen: Mohr Siebeck, 1984.

————. "Toward the Renewal of New Testament Christology." *New Testament Studies* 32 (1986): 362–77.

Kermode, Frank. *The Genesis of Secrecy: On the Interpretation of Narrative.* Cambridge, Mass.: Harvard University Press, 1979.

Kerr, Alan R. *The Temple of Jesus' Body: The Temple Theme in the Gospel of John.* Journal for the Study of the New Testament: Supplement Series 220. London: Sheffield Academic, 2002.

Klayman, Seth. "Sukkoth from the Tanakh to Tannaitic Texts: Exegetical Traditions, Emergent Rituals, and Eschatological Associations." Ph.D. diss., Duke University, 2008.

Köstenberger, Andreas. "John." In *Commentary on the New Testament Use of the Old Testament,* edited by G. K. Beale and D. A. Carson, 415–21. Grand Rapids: Baker Academic, 2007.

Kupp, David D. *Matthew's Emmanuel: Divine Presence and God's People in the First Gospel.* Society for New Testament Studies Monograph Series 90. Cambridge: Cambridge University Press, 1996.

Lane, William L. *The Gospel according to Mark.* New International Commentary on the New Testament. Grand Rapids: Eerdmans, 1974.

Lindars, Barnabas. *New Testament Apologetic: The Doctrinal Significance of the Old Testament Quotations.* Philadelphia: Westminster, 1961.

Litwak, Kenneth D. *Echoes of Scripture in Luke-Acts: Telling the Story of God's People Intertextually.* Journal for the Study of the New Testament: Supplement Series 282. London: T&T Clark, 2005.

Lodge, David. *Small World: An Academic Romance.* London: Secker & Warburg, 1984.

Luther, Martin. "Preface to the Old Testament." In *Luther's Works,* vol. 35, edited by E. Theodore Bachmann, 235–36. Philadelphia: Muhlenberg, 1960.

Luz, Ulrich. *Matthew 1–7: A Commentary.* Edinburgh: T&T Clark, 1989.

Marcus, Joel. "Identity and Ambiguity in Markan Christology." In Gaventa and Hays, *Seeking the Identity,* 133–47.

————. *Mark: A New Translation with Introduction and Commentary.* 2 vols. Anchor Bible 27 and 27A. New York: Doubleday, 2000–2009.

————. *The Way of the Lord: Christological Exegesis of the Old Testament in the Gospel of Mark.* Louisville, Ky.: Westminster John Knox, 1992.

Mason, Anita. *The Illusionist.* London: Abacus, 1983.

Meier, John P. "The Historical Jesus and the Historical Sabbath." In *Redefining First-Century Jewish and Christian Identities: Essays in Honor of Ed Parish Sanders,* edited by Fabian Udoh et al., 297–307. Notre Dame, Ind.: University of Notre Dame Press, 2008.

Menken, M. J. J. *Matthew's Bible: The Old Testament Text of the Evangelist.* Bibliotheca ephemeridum theologicarum lovaniensium 173. Leuven: Peeters, 2004.

———. *Old Testament Quotations in the Fourth Gospel: Studies in Textual Form.* Kampen: Kok Pharos, 1996.

Miller, Arthur. Quoted by Richard Eyre in his director's notes for the *Playbill* for the Broadway production of *The Crucible*, 2001.

Minear, Paul S. *The Good News according to Matthew: A Training Manual for Prophets.* St. Louis: Chalice, 2000.

———. "The Original Functions of John 21." *Journal of Biblical Literature* 102 (1983): 85–98.

Moberly, R. W. L. *The Bible, Theology, and Faith: A Study of Abraham and Jesus.* Cambridge Studies in Christian Doctrine. Cambridge: Cambridge University Press, 2000. See esp. "Jesus in Matthew's Gospel as Son of God."

Moessner, David P. "'Abraham Saw My Day': Making Greater Sense of John 8:48-59 from the LXX Version than the MT Genesis 22." In *Die Septuaginta und das frühe Christentum*, edited by Thomas S. Caulley and Hermann Lichtenberger, 329–38. Tübingen: Mohr Siebeck, 2011.

———. "Luke's 'Plan of God' from the Greek Psalter: The Rhetorical Thrust of 'the Prophets and the Psalms' in Peter's Speech at Pentecost." In *Scripture and Traditions: Essays on Early Judaism and Christianity in Honor of Carl R. Holladay*, edited by Patrick Gray and Gail R. O'Day, 223–38. Supplements to Novum Testamentum 129. Leiden: Brill, 2008.

Moule, C. F. D. "The Christology of Acts." In *Studies in Luke-Acts*, edited by Leander E. Keck and J. Louis Martyn, 159–85. Nashville: Abingdon, 1966.

Oden, Thomas C., and Christopher A. Hall, eds. *Mark.* Ancient Christian Commentary on Scripture. Downers Grove, Ill.: InterVarsity, 1998.

Pao, David. *Acts and the Isaianic New Exodus.* Wissenschaftliche Untersuchungen zum Neuen Testament, Zweite Reihe, 130. Tübingen: Mohr Siebeck, 2000. Reprint, Grand Rapids: Baker Academic, 2002.

Pesch, Rudolf. *Das Markusevangelium.* Herders theologischer Kommentar zum Neuen Testament 2. Freiburg-Basel-Vienna: Herder, 1976.

Ratzinger, Joseph (Pope Benedict XVI). *Jesus of Nazareth: From the Baptism in the Jordan to the Transfiguration.* San Francisco: Ignatius Press, 2007.

Ricoeur, Paul. *Oneself as Another.* Chicago: University of Chicago Press, 1992.

Ritter, Christine. *Rachels Klage im antiken Judentum und frühen Christentum.* Arbeiten zur Geschichte des antiken Judentums und des Urchristentums 52. Leiden: Brill, 2003.

Rowe, C. Kavin. "Acts 2:36 and the Continuity of Lukan Christology." *New Testament Studies* 53 (2007): 37–56.

————. *Early Narrative Christology: The Lord in the Gospel of Luke.* Beihefte zur Zeitschrift für die neutestamentliche Wissenschaft 139. Berlin: de Gruyter, 2006. Reprint, Grand Rapids: Baker Academic, 2009.

————. "Luke and the Trinity: An Essay in Ecclesial Biblical Theology." *Scottish Journal of Theology* 56 (2003): 1–26.

Sanders, E. P. *The Historical Figure of Jesus.* London: Penguin, 1993.

————. *Jesus and Judaism.* Philadelphia: Fortress, 1985.

Schnelle, Udo. *Theology of the New Testament.* Grand Rapids: Baker, 2009. German original: *Theologie des Neuen Testaments.* Göttingen: Vandenhoeck & Ruprecht, 2007.

Schreiber, Johannes. *Die Markuspassion: Eine redaktionsgeschichtliche Untersuchung.* Beihefte zur Zeitschrift für die neutestamentliche Wissenschaft 68. Berlin: de Gruyter, 1993.

Schuchard, Bruce G. *Scripture within Scripture: The Interrelationship of Form and Function in the Explicit Old Testament Citations in the Gospel of John.* Society of Biblical Literature Dissertation Series 133. Atlanta: Scholars, 1992.

Schwermer, Anna Maria. "Der Auferstandene und die Emmausjünger." In *Auferstehung—Resurrection,* edited by Friedrich Avemarie and Hermann Lichtenberger, 95–117. Tübingen: Mohr Siebeck, 2001.

Segal, Alan F. *Two Powers in Heaven: Early Rabbinic Reports about Christianity and Gnosticism.* Studies in Judaism in Late Antiquity. Leiden: Brill, 1977. Reprint, Waco, Tex.: Baylor University Press, 2012.

Segal, David. "In Letter, Warren Buffett Concedes a Tough Year." *New York Times,* February 28, 2009, http://www.nytimes.com/2009/03/01/business/01buffett.html.

Senior, Donald. "The Lure of the Formula Quotations: Re-assessing Matthew's Use of the Old Testament with the Passion Narrative as a Test Case." In *The Scriptures in the Gospels,* edited by Christopher Mark Tuckett, 89–115. Bibliotheca ephemeridum theologicarum lovaniensium 131. Leuven: Leuven University Press, 1997.

Soares Prabhu, George M. *The Formula Quotations in the Infancy Narrative of Matthew.* Analecta biblica 63. Rome: Biblical Institute, 1976.

Stanton, Graham N. "The Fourfold Gospel." *New Testament Studies* 43 (1997): 317–46.

————. *The Gospels and Jesus.* 2nd ed. New York: Oxford University Press, 2002.

Streett, Andrew. *The Vine and the Son of Man: Eschatological Interpretation of Psalm 80 in Early Judaism.* Minneapolis: Fortress, 2014.

Thompson, Marianne Meye. *The Promise of the Father: Jesus and God in the New Testament.* Louisville, Ky.: Westminster John Knox, 2000.

———. "'They Bear Witness to Me': The Psalms in the Passion Narrative of the Gospel of John." In Wagner, Rowe, and Grieb, *Word Leaps the Gap*, 267–83.

Tuckett, Christopher M. "The Christology of Luke-Acts." In *The Unity of Luke-Acts*, edited by Joseph Verheyden, 133–64. Bibliotheca ephemeridum theologicarum lovaniensium 142. Leuven: Leuven University Press, 1999.

———, ed. *The Scriptures in the Gospels*. Bibliotheca ephemeridum theologicarum lovaniensium 131. Leuven: Leuven University Press, 1997.

Turner, Max. "'Trinitarian' Pneumatology in the New Testament? Towards an Explanation of the Worship of Jesus." *Asbury Theological Journal* 57 (2002): 167–86.

Wagner, J. Ross. *Heralds of Salvation: Paul and Isaiah "In Concert" in Romans 9–11*. Supplements to Novum Testamentum 101. Leiden: Brill, 2002.

———. *Reading the Sealed Book: Old Greek Isaiah and the Problem of Septuagint Hermeneutics*. Forschungen zum Alten Testament 88. Tübingen: Mohr Siebeck, 2013. Waco, Tex.: Baylor University Press, 2013.

Wagner, J. Ross, C. Kavin Rowe, and A. Katherine Grieb, eds. *The Word Leaps the Gap: Essays on Scripture and Theology in Honor of Richard B. Hays*. Grand Rapids: Eerdmans, 2008.

Watson, Francis. *Gospel Writing: A Canonical Perspective*. Grand Rapids: Eerdmans, 2013.

———. *Paul and the Hermeneutics of Faith*. London: T&T Clark, 2004.

Watts, Rikk E. *Isaiah's New Exodus and Mark*. Wissenschaftliche Untersuchungen zum Neuen Testament 2. Reihe 88. Tübingen: Mohr Siebeck, 1997.

Williams, Rowan. *Christ on Trial: How the Gospel Unsettles Our Judgement*. London: Fount, 2000.

———. *The Wound of Knowledge: A Theological History from the New Testament to Luther and St. John of the Cross*. Eugene, Ore.: Wipf & Stock, 1998.

Wood, James. "Victory Speech." *New Yorker*, November 17, 2008.

Wright, N. T. *How God Became King: The Forgotten Story of the Gospels*. New York: HarperOne, 2012.

———. *Jesus and the Victory of God*. London: SPCK, 1996. Minneapolis: Fortress, 1996.

CREDITS

I would like to thank the journal *Pro Ecclesia* for permission to include and adapt (in chaps. 1 and 2) some material that originally appeared in my essay "Can the Gospels Teach Us to Read the Old Testament?" *Pro Ecclesia* 11 (2002): 402–18. Likewise, I offer thanks to Cambridge University Press for permission to incorporate some material from my article "The Canonical Matrix of the Gospels," in *The Cambridge Companion to the Gospels* (ed. Stephen C. Barton; Cambridge: Cambridge University Press, 2006), 53–75. Portions of my Matthew chapter were adapted from my article in the South African journal *HTS Teologiese Studies/Theological Studies*: "The Gospel of Matthew: Reconfigured Torah," *HTS Theological Studies* 61, nos. 1–2 (2005): 165–90. My chapter on the Gospel of Luke has adapted a few paragraphs from my essay "Reading the Bible with Eyes of Faith: The Practice of Theological Exegesis," *Journal of Theological Interpretation* 1 (2007): 5–21. And my John chapter has adapted a short passage from my essay "The Materiality of John's Symbolic World," in *Preaching John's Gospel: The World It Imagines* (ed. David Fleer and David Bland; St. Louis: Chalice, 2008), 5–12. I am grateful to these journals and publishers for their permission to reproduce and/or adapt the content of these earlier attempts to explore aspects of the Evangelists' use of Israel's Scripture.

Index of Scriptural References

Other Ancient Writings

Pseudepigrapha

Mishnah

Nag Hammadi Codices

INDEX OF NAMES